JASPER WILDE

From Poodles to Doodles

A Beginners Guide to Poodle Mixes

First published by XPress Publishing 2023

Copyright © 2023 by Jasper Wilde

All rights reserved. No part of this publication may be reproduced, stored or transmitted in any form or by any means, electronic, mechanical, photocopying, recording, scanning, or otherwise without written permission from the publisher. It is illegal to copy this book, post it to a website, or distribute it by any other means without permission.

Jasper Wilde asserts the moral right to be identified as the author of this work.

Jasper Wilde has no responsibility for the persistence or accuracy of URLs for external or third-party Internet Websites referred to in this publication and does not guarantee that any content on such Websites is, or will remain, accurate or appropriate.

Designations used by companies to distinguish their products are often claimed as trademarks. All brand names and product names used in this book and on its cover are trade names, service marks, trademarks and registered trademarks of their respective owners. The publishers and the book are not associated with any product or vendor mentioned in this book. None of the companies referenced within the book have endorsed the book.

The Second Edition was created solely to update the trim size to be more consistent with most other paperbacks.

Second edition

This book was professionally typeset on Reedsy.
Find out more at reedsy.com

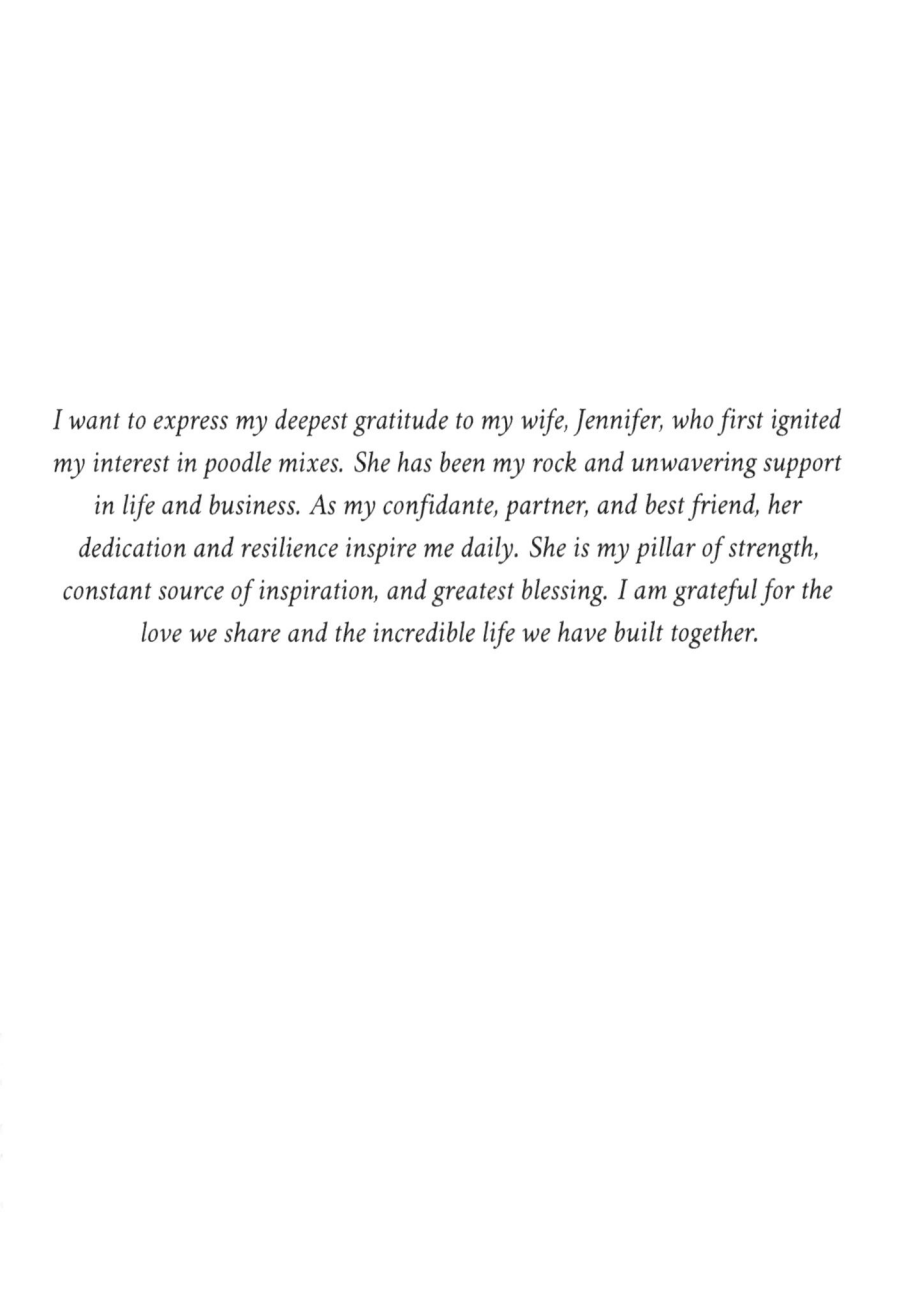

I want to express my deepest gratitude to my wife, Jennifer, who first ignited my interest in poodle mixes. She has been my rock and unwavering support in life and business. As my confidante, partner, and best friend, her dedication and resilience inspire me daily. She is my pillar of strength, constant source of inspiration, and greatest blessing. I am grateful for the love we share and the incredible life we have built together.

"No matter how little money and how few possessions you own, having a dog makes you rich."

- Louis Sabin

Contents

Preface	iii
Poodles: Where it all begins	1
Welcome the Poodle Hybrids	8
Aussiedoodle	10
Bernedoodle	14
Bichonpoo aka Bichpoo	19
Boxerdoodle	26
Cavapoo, aka Cavoodle	31
Cavapoochon	37
Cockapoo	44
Cockapoochon	50
Corgipoo	55
Danoodle	61
Doodleman	69
Goldendoodle	75
Irish Doodle	81
Labradoodle	87
Maltipoo	92
Newfypoo	99
Pinny-poo	106
Pomapoo	112
Pomapoochon	117
Pomskydoodle	123
Saint Berndoodle	128

Schnoodle aka Schnoodlepoo aka Snickerdoodle	134
Sheepadoodle aka Sheepapoo	139
Shihpoo	145
Westiepoo	152
Whoodle	160
Yorkiepoo	166
Yorkiepoochon	172
Conclusion	177

Preface

Welcome to the enchanting world of poodle hybrids! What started out to be a short digest for friends and family became a much longer project once I explored the breadth of these breeds. In this book, aptly titled "From Poodles to Doodles," my aim is to provide you with a comprehensive yet concise exploration of the remarkable realm of poodle crosses. This book is primarily written for my friends who frequently inquire about the intriguing nature of hybrids like my favorite, the Cavapoochon. However, it is also designed to serve as a valuable quick reference for anyone fascinated by the diverse world of doodles.

Allow me to clarify the scope of this book from the outset. "From Poodles to Doodles" is not an exhaustive encyclopedia encompassing every poodle hybrid or an extensive guide to poodle care. Instead, it is a consolidation of some of the most popular hybrids, presented as a convenient resource for enthusiasts seeking a swift introduction to these delightful breeds.

Within the pages of this book, you may stumble upon a hybrid that captures your heart and resonates with your lifestyle. Perhaps, you will discover the perfect companion to join your family and add joy to your everyday life. Whether you are seeking a hypoallergenic companion or a playful partner, there is likely a poodle hybrid waiting to meet your fancy.

It is important to note that this book does not demand a cover-to-cover reading. If a particular hybrid piques your interest, feel free to navigate directly to its dedicated page for a focused and immersive exploration. Because of this, you will find some repetition with the many pages. While some hybrids require the same care, others may have a nuance here or there.

It is worth mentioning that while I have strived to include images of as many hybrids as possible, some may lack visual representation. Certain hybrids are rare and more elusive, making it challenging to find royalty pictures, especially considering the global nature of their breeding. But fear not, for the descriptions and information provided will help you envision their unique qualities and characteristics.

As I embarked on this project, I was astounded by the sheer multitude of poodle hybrids that exist. I found myself delightfully immersed in their captivating world, and it is my hope that you, too, will revel in the discovery of these extraordinary breeds. "From Poodles to Doodles" offers an invitation to expand your knowledge, embrace diversity, and perhaps even inspire the adoption of a furry companion that resonates with your soul.

So, without further ado, let us embark on this journey together, exploring the wonderful universe of poodle hybrids. May you find joy, knowledge, and a sense of wonder within these pages, just as I did while writing this book.

Poodles: Where it all begins

History of the Poodle

The poodle is a breed with a rich history that traces back several centuries. While the exact origins of the breed are debated, it is widely believed to have originated in Germany, where it was known as the Pudelhund. The breed's name comes from the German word "Pudel," meaning "to splash," which reflects the breed's excellent water retrieving abilities.

Poodles were initially bred as water retrievers, primarily used for retrieving waterfowl during hunting expeditions. Their distinctive grooming style, with the characteristic pom-poms and shaved areas, originated as a practical means to enhance their swimming abilities while keeping vital organs and joints warm in cold water.

The Three Primary Sizes of the Breed and Their Origins

Poodles come in three primary sizes: Standard, Miniature, and Toy. Each size has its unique characteristics and history.

1. Standard Poodle: The largest of the three sizes, the Standard Poodle, has a height exceeding 15 inches (38 cm). They were

originally bred as hunting dogs and were highly valued for their intelligence and versatility in various tasks. Standard Poodles were commonly used to retrieve waterfowl and were excellent at tracking and scent work.
2. Miniature Poodle: The Miniature Poodle stands between 10 and 15 inches (25-38 cm) in height. They were developed by selectively breeding smaller Standard Poodles, primarily for companionship and to serve as delightful household pets. Miniature Poodles possess the same intelligence and trainability as their larger counterparts.
3. Toy Poodle: The Toy Poodle is the smallest of the three sizes, standing under 10 inches (25 cm) in height. They were bred down in size from the Miniature Poodle and were primarily kept as companions and lap dogs. Toy Poodles are renowned for their elegance, charm, and delightful personalities.

What is Unique about the Poodle

The poodle, a breed known for its many distinguishing characteristics, stands out in the canine world for more than just its unmistakable coif. The poodle's hypoallergenic coat, a dense, curly covering that sheds minimally, is one of its most admired characteristics, endearing them to many who suffer from allergies or are sensitive to pet dander. Their kind exterior conceals a strong intelligence; they are among the most smart canine breeds. Their excellent problem-solving abilities, along with an instinctive desire to please their owners, make them not only trainable but also suitable candidates for professions ranging from therapeutic companions to nimble sport participation. The tremendous adaptability of poodles is what truly distinguishes them. They adapt and excel in a variety of situations, whether it's retrieving in the wild, competing in a rally, or navigating city life, making them ideal partners for a wide range of lifestyles and environments.

Temperament and Personality of the Poodle

Poodles are praised for their fascinating personalities and charming disposition in addition to their attractive appearance, which is why they have been favorite companions for so many years. They are known for being gregarious and value human company. They develop strong ties with their families and are friendly to strangers as well. Their friendly demeanor blends well with their alertness; they are constantly vigilant and full of activity. Regular physical and mental activity is essential to ensuring that they remain at their happiest, preventing any signs of boredom. However, this energetic exterior conceals a heart that is rife with humorous mischief. Poodles enjoy playing energetic games and retain their young vigor well into age. They frequently delight their owners with their adorable antics and mischievous sense of humor.

FROM POODLES TO DOODLES

Standard Poodle

Height: 18-24 inches
Weight: 50-70 lbs
Lifespan: 12-15 years
Intelligence: High
Energy Level: Hyper
Vocal Level: Frequent
Coat Length: curly, long, medium, short
Other traits: easy to train, hypoallergenic, loves water, requires lots of grooming, strong loyalty tendencies, tolerates being alone

Minature Poodle

Height: 10-15 inches
Weight: 10-15 lbs
Lifespan: 10-18 years
Intelligence: High
Energy Level: Hyper
Vocal Level: Frequent
Coat Length: curly, long, medium, short
Other traits: easy to train, hypoallergenic, loves water, requires lots of grooming, strong loyalty tendencies

Toy Poodle

Height: 6-10 inches
Weight: 4-6 lbs
Lifespan: 12-18 years
Intelligence: High
Energy Level: Calm
Vocal Level: When necessary
Coat Length: curly, medium
Other traits: apartment-friendly, cold weather tolerant, easy to train, good for first-time pet owners, hot weather tolerant

Care including Feeding, Exercise, Grooming, Health Problems

Proper care is crucial to ensure the well-being of poodles. Here are some aspects to consider:

1. Feeding: Provide a balanced diet suitable for your poodle's age, size, and activity level. Consult with a veterinarian to determine the appropriate type and amount of food to maintain optimal health.
2. Exercise: Poodles are active dogs that require regular exercise to prevent restlessness and obesity. Aim for daily walks, playtime, and mental stimulation activities. Engaging them in dog sports or agility training can also be beneficial.
3. Grooming: Poodles have a continuously growing, curly coat that requires regular grooming to prevent matting. Regular brushing, professional trimming, and occasional bathing are necessary. Many poodle owners opt for professional grooming services to maintain the breed's distinctive appearance.
4. Health Problems: While poodles are generally healthy dogs, they can be prone to certain health issues. These may include hip dysplasia, progressive retinal atrophy (PRA), patellar luxation, epilepsy, and certain skin conditions. Regular veterinary check-ups and responsible breeding practices can help minimize these risks.

Training

Poodles are renowned for their exceptional intelligence and eagerness to learn, making them highly trainable canines that actively seek to satisfy their owners. Essential training guidelines for these dogs emphasize the use of positive reinforcement, like treats and praise, to instill desired behaviors. Consistency in setting clear rules, maintaining regular routines, and practicing patience are fundamental to their learning trajectory. Additionally, to cultivate a confident and sociable demeanor in poodles, it's vital to expose them early on to a variety of people, animals, and environments.

Benefits of the Poodle

Poodles offer several benefits as companion dogs:

1. Allergy-Friendly: Poodles' hypoallergenic coats make them suitable for individuals with allergies or sensitivities to pet dander.
2. Versatility: Poodles' intelligence and trainability make them adaptable to various activities and roles, from family pets to therapy or service dogs.
3. Loyal Companions: Poodles form strong bonds with their owners and are known for their loyalty and devotion.
4. Low Shedding: Poodles shed minimally, reducing the amount of hair and dander in the home.

Interesting Facts

1. Poodles are excellent swimmers and were historically used for water retrieving.
2. The poodle's distinctive grooming style originated from practical reasons related to their swimming abilities.
3. Poodles have been crossbred with other breeds to create popular hybrids such as the Labradoodle and Goldendoodle.
4. The breed is represented in various sizes, including Standard, Miniature, and Toy.
5. Poodles have been successful in a wide range of activities, includ-

ing agility, obedience, and search and rescue work.
6. They were popular among European nobility, including Louis XVI of France and Queen Victoria.
7. The poodle is the national dog of France.
8. Poodles come in a variety of coat colors, including black, white, brown, gray, apricot, and red.
9. The intelligence of poodles ranks among the highest of all dog breeds.
10. Poodles have been featured in many works of art, including paintings by artists such as Francisco Goya.

Welcome the Poodle Hybrids

Poodle hybrids, also known as "doodle" dogs, have gained significant popularity over the past few decades. These hybrids are created by crossing a Poodle with another breed, resulting in offspring that inherit traits from both parent breeds. The goal is often to combine the desirable characteristics of the Poodle, such as its intelligence and hypoallergenic coat, with the traits of the other breed.

The history of poodle hybrids can be traced back to the late 20th century when breeders began crossing Poodles with other breeds to create dogs with specific traits. One of the earliest and most well-known Poodle hybrids is the Labradoodle, which was first developed in Australia in the 1980s. The goal was to produce a guide dog that was hypoallergenic and had a temperament suitable for people with disabilities. Labradoodles are a cross between a Poodle and a Labrador Retriever and have gained popularity worldwide due to their friendly nature and low-shedding coats.

Another popular poodle hybrid is the Goldendoodle, which is a cross between a Poodle and a Golden Retriever. They were initially bred in the 1990s as hypoallergenic and trainable guide dogs. Goldendoodles are known for their friendly and social personalities, as well as their wavy or curly, low-shedding coats.

Since the introduction of Labradoodles and Goldendoodles, many other Poodle hybrids have emerged, each with its own unique name and characteristics. Some examples include:

1. Cockapoo: A cross between a Poodle and a Cocker Spaniel. Cockapoos are known for their friendly nature, intelligence, and low-shedding coats.
2. Bernedoodle: A cross between a Poodle and a Bernese Mountain Dog. Bernedoodles are often sought after for their playful and affectionate temperament, as well as their wavy or curly coats.
3. Aussiedoodle: A cross between a Poodle and an Australian Shepherd. Aussiedoodles are typically energetic, intelligent, and highly trainable. They often have wavy or curly coats.
4. Sheepadoodle: A cross between a Poodle and an Old English Sheepdog. Sheepadoodles are known for their loyal and protective nature. They often have a wavy or curly coat that requires regular grooming.

These are just a few examples of the many Poodle hybrids that have been developed over the years. The popularity of these hybrids continues to grow due to their desirable traits, such as hypoallergenic coats, intelligence, and friendly personalities. However, it's important to note that not all Poodle hybrids are guaranteed to inherit these traits, as characteristics can vary within each litter.

Let's jump in and look more in-depth at some of the most popular poodle hybrids.

Aussiedoodle

History of the Aussiedoodle

The Aussiedoodle is a popular poodle hybrid that emerged in the late 20th century as a cross between the Australian Shepherd and the Poodle breeds. Like other designer dogs, the exact origins of the Aussiedoodle are unclear, but it is believed to have originated in North America. The intentional breeding of Aussiedoodles began around the 1990s, with the aim of creating a versatile and intelligent companion with hypoallergenic traits.

What is Unique about the Aussiedoodle

The Aussiedoodle combines the intelligence and trainability of the Poodle with the herding instincts and athleticism of the Australian Shepherd. One of the unique characteristics of the Aussiedoodle is its coat, which can vary from curly to wavy, and it can come in a variety of colors. This breed is highly sought after for its hypoallergenic properties, making it suitable for individuals with allergies.

Aussiedoodle / Jake Green / Unsplash.com

Temperament and Personality of the Aussiedoodle

Aussiedoodles are known for their friendly and affectionate nature. They are often described as being highly sociable, intelligent, and eager to please. This breed tends to be loyal and devoted to their families, forming strong bonds with their owners. Aussiedoodles are often good with children and other pets, making them a great choice for families. They are also known to be highly energetic and require regular exercise and mental stimulation to thrive.

Care for the Aussiedoodle

1. Feeding: Provide a balanced diet of high-quality dog food suited to their size, age, and activity level.
2. Exercise: Aussiedoodles are energetic dogs that require daily exercise to keep them mentally and physically stimulated. Regular walks, playtime, and activities such as agility training are beneficial.
3. Grooming: Their coat requires regular brushing to prevent matting and occasional professional grooming to maintain its condition. Regular nail trims and ear cleaning are also essential.
4. Health Problems: Aussiedoodles are generally considered a healthy breed. However, they may be prone to certain health issues inherited from their parent breeds, including hip dysplasia, eye problems, and allergies.

Training

Aussiedoodles are highly intelligent and trainable dogs. They excel in obedience training, agility, and other dog sports. Positive reinforcement methods, such as rewards and praise, work best with this breed.

Early socialization and consistent, firm training techniques will help them become well-rounded and obedient companions.

Benefits of the Aussiedoodle

1. Versatility: Aussiedoodles are adaptable and excel in various roles, including therapy dogs, service dogs, and family companions.
2. Hypoallergenic: Their low-shedding coat makes them suitable for individuals with allergies.
3. Intelligence: Aussiedoodles are highly intelligent, making them quick learners and easy to train.
4. Social Nature: They are typically friendly and sociable, getting along well with children, other pets, and strangers.

Interesting Facts

1. Aussiedoodles can vary in size, depending on the size of the Poodle parent—ranging from small to standard.
2. They are often referred to as "designer dogs" or "doodle dogs" due to their mixed breed status.
3. Aussiedoodles can have different coat patterns and colors, including solid, merle, and parti-colors.
4. Some Aussiedoodles may have heterochromia, meaning they have different-colored eyes.
5. This breed requires mental stimulation, and puzzle toys can help keep them entertained.
6. Aussiedoodles are known for their "smiling" expressions, with a lifted corner of their mouth that resembles a grin.

Bernedoodle

History of the Bernedoodle

The Bernedoodle is a relatively new hybrid breed that has gained popularity in recent years. It is a cross between a Bernese Mountain Dog and a Poodle, typically either a Standard Poodle or a Miniature Poodle. While the exact origins of the Bernedoodle are unclear, it is believed to have originated in the United States during the 2000s as part of the designer dog trend.

The goal of breeding Bernedoodles was to combine the desirable traits of both parent breeds. Bernese Mountain Dogs are known for their gentle nature and loyalty, while Poodles are highly intelligent and hypoallergenic. The aim was to create a dog that possessed the Bernese Mountain Dog's friendly temperament and the Poodle's hypoallergenic coat.

Bernedoodle

What is Unique about the Bernedoodle

The Bernedoodle stands out due to its distinctive appearance and coat. It inherits the wavy or curly, low-shedding coat of the Poodle, which makes it an excellent choice for individuals with allergies. The coat can come in a variety of colors, including black, brown, and white combinations, resembling the Bernese Mountain Dog's coat. This wide range of colors adds to the breed's uniqueness and visual appeal.

Temperament and Personality of the Bernedoodle

Bernedoodles are known for their friendly and affectionate nature. They are often described as being gentle, intelligent, and social dogs. With the combination of their Bernese Mountain Dog and Poodle heritage, they tend to be devoted to their families and get along well with children and other pets. Bernedoodles are typically eager to please and are quick learners, making them suitable for various training activities.

Care for the Bernedoodle

1. **Feeding:** Bernedoodles require a well-balanced diet to maintain their health. It is important to provide them with high-quality dog food that meets their nutritional needs. The specific feeding requirements may vary based on the size and activity level of the individual dog.
2. **Exercise:** Bernedoodles are energetic dogs and require regular exercise to keep them physically and mentally stimulated. Daily walks, playtime, and interactive toys can help meet their exercise needs. Providing them with opportunities for socialization and mental enrichment is also beneficial.

3. **Grooming:** The grooming needs of Bernedoodles depend on the type of coat they inherit. If they have a curly or wavy coat, regular brushing is necessary to prevent matting and to keep their fur tangle-free. Professional grooming may be required every few months to maintain a well-groomed appearance.
4. **Health Problems:** As with any dog breed, Bernedoodles can be prone to certain health issues. Some common health concerns include hip dysplasia, elbow dysplasia, progressive retinal atrophy (PRA), and certain genetic disorders inherited from their parent breeds. Regular vet check-ups, a balanced diet, and maintaining a healthy lifestyle can help minimize the risk of these problems.

Training the Bernedoodle

Training a Bernedoodle should start early and focus on positive reinforcement techniques. They are intelligent dogs and generally respond well to reward-based training methods. Early socialization is essential to help them become well-rounded and confident dogs. Consistency, patience, and using positive reinforcement techniques such as treats and praise will yield the best results.

Benefits of the Bernedoodle

The Bernedoodle offers several benefits to potential owners:

1. **Hypoallergenic:** Many Bernedoodles have a low-shedding coat, making them suitable for individuals with allergies or sensitivities to dog hair.
2. Family-Friendly: Bernedoodles are typically friendly and gentle with children and other pets, making them excellent family companions.

3. Intelligence and Trainability: With their Poodle heritage, Bernedoodles are intelligent and trainable, making them suitable for various training activities and tasks.
4. Versatility: Bernedoodles come in different sizes, ranging from miniature to standard, allowing potential owners to choose a size that fits their lifestyle and living arrangements.

Interesting Facts about the Bernedoodle

1. The Bernedoodle's name is a combination of "Bernese," referring to the Bernese Mountain Dog, and "Poodle."
2. The size of Bernedoodles can vary depending on the size of the Poodle used in the crossbreeding process. Miniature Poodles result in smaller Bernedoodles, while Standard Poodles produce larger ones.
3. Bernedoodles have gained popularity due to their hypoallergenic coat, which makes them a suitable option for individuals who typically experience allergies around dogs.
4. Bernedoodles are known for their calm and patient nature, making them good therapy dogs.
5. Some Bernedoodles inherit the Poodle's intelligence and Bernese Mountain Dog's herding instincts, which can result in a dog that excels in various canine sports and activities.
6. The first-generation Bernedoodles (F1) are the direct offspring of a Bernese Mountain Dog and a Poodle. Further breeding can create multigenerational Bernedoodles (F2, F3, etc.), which can lead to more predictable traits.
7. The popularity of Bernedoodles has led to the establishment of breed-specific rescue organizations that specialize in finding homes for Bernedoodles in need.

Bichonpoo aka Bichpoo

History of the Bichonpoo

The Bichonpoo, also known as the Bichpoo or Poochon, is a hybrid breed that combines the Bichon Frise and the Poodle. Its exact origins are not well-documented, but it is believed to have emerged in the United States during the late 20th century as breeders began crossing different purebred dogs to create new and unique breeds.

The Bichon Frise is a small, fluffy breed with a cheerful and friendly disposition. Originating in the Mediterranean, it was popular among European nobility during the Renaissance period. These dogs were often seen accompanying sailors on ships and were treasured for their lively nature and entertaining abilities.

Breeders developed the Bichonpoo with the aim of combining the desirable traits of both the Bichon Frise and the Poodle. The goal was to create a small, affectionate companion dog with a low-shedding coat, making it a suitable choice for individuals with allergies or those who preferred a low-maintenance coat.

Bichonpoo / Ursula Page / Shutterstock.com

What is Unique about the Bichonpoo

In a world filled with a myriad of dog breeds, the Bichonpoo emerges as a true standout, capturing hearts with its blend of characteristics from both the Bichon Frise and Poodle lineage. At first glance, one is immediately drawn to its teddy bear-like appearance, characterized by a soft, curly or wavy coat. This plush coat, painted in hues of white, apricot, cream, or even a melange of these colors, gracefully frames their expressive eyes and adorable button noses. The physical allure of the Bichonpoo doesn't stop at its appearance. For those grappling with allergies or sensitivities to dog hair, this breed might just be the answer to their prayers. A nod to their Poodle heritage, Bichonpoos possess a hypoallergenic coat, ensuring minimal shedding and allergen production.

Yet, what truly elevates the Bichonpoo is its innate nature. Famed for their affectionate temperament, these dogs don't just seek human companionship, they thrive on it. Their sociable personalities make them not just pets, but cherished family members, fitting seamlessly into households with individuals of all ages. Furthermore, the Bichonpoo is not just a pretty face. They carry with them the intelligence genes of both their parent breeds. This cognitive prowess makes them not only quick learners but also highly trainable companions. Whether it's obedience training or indulging in diverse canine sports, the Bichonpoo is always up for the challenge, proving time and again that they're as brainy as they are beautiful.

Temperament and Personality of the Bichonpoo

Bichonpoos, with their amiable demeanor, have effortlessly carved a niche for themselves among the many dog breeds. Central to their charm is an overflowing affection they reserve for those they hold dear. These dogs don't merely exist alongside humans; they weave themselves intricately into the fabric of family life, forming unbreakable bonds with their owners. They exude warmth, often mirroring the love they receive in full measure.

Yet, a Bichonpoo's affability isn't confined to its household. With an outgoing nature, they readily embrace the wider world, cherishing every opportunity to mingle with new faces, be it human or animal. Children, with their inherent enthusiasm, find in Bichonpoos a perfect playmate. Their zest for life manifests in a playful exuberance, making them the epicenter of joy and laughter in many households. Tug-of-war or fetch, their spirited antics promise endless hours of amusement.

But it's not all fun and games. Their intelligence is palpable, making them quick learners. Keen to please their owners, Bichonpoos often showcase their smarts during training sessions, responding best to methods steeped in positivity. And while their petite size might suggest vulnerability, they possess an uncanny alertness. With ears always perked and senses attuned, they won't hesitate to sound the alarm, ensuring their loved ones are always in the know of any potential intruders or unforeseen events. In the end, the Bichonpoo emerges not just as a pet, but a trusted companion, protector, and above all, a cherished family member.

Care for the Bichonpoo

1. Feeding: Bichonpoos should be fed a well-balanced diet that is appropriate for their size, age, and activity level. It is important to provide them with high-quality dog food that meets their nutritional needs. Consult with your veterinarian for specific feeding recommendations.
2. Exercise: Although Bichonpoos are small dogs, they still require regular exercise to keep them physically and mentally stimulated. Daily walks, playtime, and interactive toys can help meet their exercise needs. They also enjoy participating in activities such as agility or obedience training.
3. Grooming: Bichonpoos have a curly or wavy coat that requires regular grooming to prevent matting and keep their fur tangle-free. They should be brushed several times a week and may require professional grooming every few months. Regular trimming of their nails, cleaning their ears, and maintaining good dental hygiene is also important.
4. Health Problems: Like all dog breeds, Bichonpoos can be prone

to certain health issues. Some common health concerns include dental problems, eye conditions, skin allergies, and joint issues. Regular veterinary check-ups, a balanced diet, and maintaining a healthy weight can help minimize the risk of these problems.

Training the Bichonpoo

When welcoming a Bichonpoo into your life, early training becomes the cornerstone of molding their journey from a bubbly puppy to a well-mannered adult dog. These dogs, with their sparkling eyes and curly fur, come packed with intelligence and a desire to please their humans. Here's how you can guide them to become the best version of themselves.

First and foremost, the mantra for Bichonpoo training is 'positive reinforcement.' These little creatures flourish under an umbrella of kindness and rewards. When they exhibit the behavior you desire, be it a simple sit or a more complex trick, let the shower of treats, praises, and affectionate pats rain down on them. This instills a positive association with good behavior, making them more inclined to repeat it. On the flip side, avoid the trap of harsh punishments. Negative methods can lead to resistance or fear, hindering the bond you're aiming to build.

Socialization is the next pivotal chapter in your Bichonpoo's life story. This world is vast and varied, and the earlier they're exposed to its diversity, the better. Whether it's a gentle toddler, a chirpy bird, or the bustling ambiance of a local market, every new encounter shapes their personality. These exposures ensure your Bichonpoo grows to be adaptable and confident, irrespective of the setting.

With their sharp intellect, Bichonpoos are primed for obedience training. Their eagerness to please serves as an added bonus, making the learning process smoother. However, the keys here are consistency and patience. Basic commands, like "sit", "stay", and "come", form the foundation. Using positive reinforcement techniques, as previously mentioned, will undoubtedly bear fruit in this venture.

Finally, the task that tests most new pet parents: housetraining. Here, routine is your best ally. Regular potty breaks combined with a steady stream of praise when they do their business in the right spot will set them on the path to success. Remember, patience is essential; every pup has its own learning curve. In sum, training your Bichonpoo is less about teaching and more about building a relationship. With the right techniques and a dash of love, you'll witness the growth of a loyal, well-behaved, and joyful canine companion.

Benefits of the Bichonpoo

The Bichonpoo offers several benefits to potential owners:

1. Hypoallergenic Coat: Many Bichonpoos have a low-shedding and hypoallergenic coat, making them suitable for individuals with allergies or sensitivities to dog hair.
2. Companionable Nature: Bichonpoos are known for their affectionate and friendly personalities, making them great companions for individuals or families of all ages.
3. Trainability: With their intelligence and eagerness to please, Bichonpoos are generally easy to train. They can excel in obedience training and enjoy learning new tricks.
4. Adaptability: Bichonpoos are adaptable dogs that can thrive in various living situations, including apartments or houses with or without a yard. Their small size makes them suitable for urban

environments.

Interesting Facts about the Bichonpoo

1. Crossbreeding the Bichon Frise and the Poodle resulted in the creation of the Bichonpoo, a breed that combines the best traits of both parent breeds.
2. Bichonpoos come in a variety of coat colors, including white, cream, apricot, and other combinations.
3. Bichonpoos are known for their teddy bear-like appearance, which contributes to their popularity as companion dogs.
4. The Bichonpoo's hypoallergenic coat makes them a suitable option for individuals who typically experience allergies around dogs.
5. Bichonpoos are generally sociable and get along well with children and other pets, making them great family pets.
6. These dogs have a playful and energetic nature, and they enjoy participating in activities that engage their minds and bodies.
7. Bichonpoos may vary in size, depending on the size of the Poodle parent. They can range from small to medium-sized dogs.
8. Bichonpoos are often seen in therapy and service dog roles due to their friendly and gentle temperament.
9. Bichonpoos are known for their longevity and can live for 12 to 15 years or even longer with proper care.
10. The popularity of Bichonpoos has led to the establishment of breed-specific rescue organizations that specialize in finding homes for Bichonpoos in need.

Boxerdoodle

History of the Boxerdoodle

The Boxerdoodle, also known as the Boxerpoo or Boxerdoodle Retriever, is a hybrid breed that combines the Boxer and the Poodle. While the exact origins of the Boxerdoodle are unclear, it is believed to have emerged in the United States as part of the designer dog trend. The goal of breeding Boxerdoodles was to combine the desirable traits of both parent breeds, creating a dog with the Boxer's athleticism and loyalty, as well as the Poodle's intelligence and hypoallergenic coat.

What is Unique about the Boxerdoodle

The Boxerdoodle, a striking blend of the robust Boxer and the sophisticated Poodle, boasts a myriad of characteristics that make it uniquely captivating. Their appearance is a delightful tapestry of genes, oscillating between the muscular prowess of the Boxer and the refined elegance of the Poodle, all enveloped in a coat that ranges from gentle waves to tight curls. This often hypoallergenic coat offers a respite to allergy sufferers. Beyond their looks, Boxerdoodles are a whirlwind of energy and athleticism, inheriting the Boxer's zeal for play and activity.

However, their true genius lies in their intellect, a gift from their Poodle lineage. This intelligence, coupled with their innate curiosity, makes them both adaptable and eager participants in a myriad of training endeavors.

Boxerdoodle / The PhotoGuys / Shutterstock.com

Temperament and Personality of the Boxerdoodle

Boxerdoodles seamlessly combine the best traits of the Boxer and Poodle, resulting in a breed characterized by a heart full of devotion and an ever-watchful eye. At the core of a Boxerdoodle lies an unyielding loyalty; they cultivate deep bonds with their human counterparts, making them fiercely protective and always ready to stand by their side. Their zest for life is palpable, evident in their spirited playfulness and boundless energy. These traits make them ideal companions for those who love an invigorating game of fetch or long walks in the park. Their affable nature extends beyond their human family; with the right socialization, they emerge as gentle giants around children, displaying remarkable patience and care. Moreover, their keen senses and alert disposition mean that while they are playing with the family during the day, by night, they are vigilant sentinels, ever ready to safeguard their loved ones from any unforeseen threats.

Care for the Boxerdoodle

1. Feeding: Boxerdoodles should be fed a well-balanced diet that suits their age, size, and activity level. It is important to provide them with high-quality dog food that meets their nutritional needs. Consult with your veterinarian for specific feeding recommendations.
2. Exercise: Boxerdoodles are energetic dogs that require regular exercise to prevent boredom and maintain their physical and mental well-being. Daily walks, play sessions, and interactive toys can help meet their exercise needs.
3. Grooming: Boxerdoodles typically have a low-shedding coat that requires regular brushing to prevent matting and keep their fur healthy. The frequency of grooming depends on the coat type and length. They may require professional grooming occasionally to maintain their appearance.
4. Health Problems: As with any dog breed, Boxerdoodles can be prone to certain health issues. Some common health concerns may include hip dysplasia, heart problems, allergies, and certain genetic conditions inherited from their parent breeds. Regular veterinary check-ups, a balanced diet, and exercise can help minimize the

risk of these problems.

Training the Boxerdoodle

The Boxerdoodle is a delightful breed that can be trained effectively, especially when a puppy is involved. Positive reinforcement is crucial, as they quickly understand and appreciate reward-based techniques. Encouraging obedience and socialization is essential for shaping a Boxerdoodle's temperament. Exposure to various environments, people, and animals from a young age helps nurture adaptability and balance. Consistency in training is essential, with short but frequent sessions and repetition of commands. By combining patience, consistency, and positive reinforcement, a Boxerdoodle can become a well-trained and delightful companion.

Benefits of the Boxerdoodle

The Boxerdoodle offers several benefits to potential owners:

1. Hypoallergenic Coat: Many Boxerdoodles have a low-shedding and hypoallergenic coat, making them suitable for individuals with allergies or sensitivities to dog hair.
2. Energetic and Playful: Boxerdoodles have an energetic and playful nature, making them great companions for active individuals or families.
3. Loyalty and Protective Nature: These dogs are known for their loyalty and protective instincts. They can form strong bonds with their owners and provide a sense of security.
4. Trainability: Boxerdoodles are intelligent and trainable, making them suitable for various training activities and tasks.

Interesting Facts about the Boxerdoodle

1. The Boxerdoodle's name is a combination of "Boxer," referring to the Boxer breed, and "Poodle."
2. Boxerdoodles can come in a variety of coat colors, including black, brown, white, or combinations thereof.
3. They often have a sturdy build with well-defined muscles, similar to the Boxer parent.
4. Boxerdoodles are known for their expressive and alert eyes.
5. Some Boxerdoodles may exhibit protective instincts and make excellent watchdogs.
6. The size of Boxerdoodles can vary, depending on the size of the Poodle parent used in the crossbreeding process.
7. Boxerdoodles are generally sociable and enjoy being part of the family. They thrive on human companionship and attention.
8. They have a moderate to high exercise requirement and enjoy activities that engage their minds and bodies.
9. Boxerdoodles can excel in various canine sports and activities, including obedience, agility, and even therapy work.
10. The popularity of Boxerdoodles has grown in recent years due to their desirable traits and hypoallergenic coat, making them a sought-after hybrid breed.

Cavapoo, aka Cavoodle

History of the Cavapoo

The Cavapoo, also known as the Cavoodle, is a popular hybrid breed that originated in the late 1990s. It is a cross between a Cavalier King Charles Spaniel and a Poodle, typically a Miniature or Toy Poodle. The exact origins of the Cavapoo are not well-documented, but it is believed to have emerged in Australia, where it gained significant popularity before spreading to other parts of the world.

The breeding of Cavapoos was initially done with the intention of creating a companion dog that combined the desirable traits of both parent breeds. The Cavalier King Charles Spaniel is known for its friendly and affectionate nature, while the Poodle brings intelligence and hypoallergenic qualities to the mix. Breeders aimed to create a dog with a gentle temperament, low-shedding coat, and overall versatility as a family pet.

What is Unique about the Cavapoo

The Cavapoo, a delightful blend of the Cavalier King Charles Spaniel and Poodle, boasts several distinct features that endear them to many dog lovers. One of their most striking characteristics is the immense variety in their coat. Not only can their coats be wavy, curly, or straight, but they also come in a myriad of colors, from solid shades like black, brown, or apricot, to captivating combinations. This diversity ensures that no two Cavapoos are precisely alike in appearance, enhancing their charm. Moreover, their Poodle heritage grants them a potential hypoallergenic quality. Many Cavapoos possess a low-shedding coat, making them a preferable choice for individuals prone to allergies or those sensitive to pet dander. But it doesn't end with their coat. The Cavapoo also offers variety in size. Depending on whether they're bred with a Miniature or Toy Poodle, these dogs can range from the slightly larger, robust build to a petite and delicate stature, giving potential owners the flexibility to choose a companion best suited to their living situation and lifestyle preferences.

Cavapoo / Mia Anderson / Unsplash.com

Temperament and Personality of the Cavapoo

Cavapoos are known for their affectionate and friendly nature, making them excellent companions. They often inherit the loving and gentle temperament of the Cavalier King Charles Spaniel, combined with the intelligence and trainability of the Poodle. Cavapoos are typically sociable, getting along well with children, other pets, and strangers alike. They thrive on human companionship and are often described as eager to please, making them suitable for families of all sizes.

Care for the Cavapoo

1. Feeding: Cavapoos require a balanced diet to maintain their overall health and well-being. High-quality dog food, either com-

mercial or homemade, should be provided in appropriate portions based on the dog's size, age, and activity level. Consultation with a veterinarian can help determine the best diet for your Cavapoo.
2. Exercise: While Cavapoos are not excessively energetic, they still require regular exercise to keep them physically and mentally stimulated. Daily walks, play sessions, and interactive toys can help fulfill their exercise needs. Additionally, they enjoy spending time with their owners and participating in activities such as obedience training, agility, or even therapy work.
3. Grooming: The grooming needs of Cavapoos depend on their coat type. Regular brushing is recommended to prevent matting and keep their fur clean and tangle-free. If the Cavapoo has a curly or wavy coat, professional grooming may be required every few months to maintain a well-groomed appearance. Regular ear cleaning, teeth brushing, and nail trimming are also important aspects of their grooming routine.
4. Health Problems: As with any dog breed, Cavapoos can be prone to certain health issues. While crossbreeding can reduce the risk of inherited diseases, some common health concerns in Cavapoos include heart conditions, eye problems, hip dysplasia, and patellar luxation. Regular veterinary check-ups, vaccinations, a balanced diet, and a healthy lifestyle can help minimize the risk of these problems.

Training the Cavapoo

Cavapoos are intelligent dogs that generally respond well to positive reinforcement training methods. They are eager to please their owners and enjoy learning new commands and tricks. Early socialization and training are important to ensure they grow up to be well-rounded and confident dogs. Consistency, patience, and rewards such as treats and praise are effective tools in training Cavapoos. Obedience training, as well as mental stimulation activities like puzzle toys, can keep them mentally engaged and prevent boredom.

Benefits of the Cavapoo

The Cavapoo offers several benefits to potential owners:

1. Companion Qualities: Cavapoos are highly affectionate, loyal, and devoted to their families. They thrive on human companionship and make excellent family pets, providing love and companionship to people of all ages.
2. Hypoallergenic Coat: Many Cavapoos have a low-shedding coat, making them suitable for individuals with allergies or sensitivities to pet dander. While no dog is truly hypoallergenic, the reduced shedding in Cavapoos can minimize allergic reactions.
3. Adaptability: Cavapoos adapt well to different living situations, whether in apartments or larger homes. They are generally adaptable to varying lifestyles and can adjust to the activity levels and routines of their owners.
4. Trainability: With their Poodle heritage, Cavapoos are intelligent and trainable. They are quick learners and enjoy participating in training activities, which makes them suitable for obedience training, agility, and other dog sports.

Interesting Facts about the Cavapoo

1. Cavapoos are sometimes referred to as "designer dogs" due to their intentional crossbreeding and the popularity of hybrid breeds.
2. The Cavapoo's name is a combination of "Cavalier" and "Poodle," reflecting its parent breeds.

3. Cavapoos are known for their charming and expressive eyes, often inherited from the Cavalier King Charles Spaniel.
4. Some Cavapoos inherit the Poodle's curly coat, while others have a wavy or straight coat, resulting in a range of grooming requirements.
5. The size of a Cavapoo can vary significantly depending on the size of the Poodle parent used in the breeding process.
6. Cavapoos are generally sociable and enjoy being around people and other animals. They thrive on attention and affection.
7. Due to their adorable appearance and gentle nature, Cavapoos have become popular therapy dogs, providing comfort and support in various settings.
8. Cavapoos are known to have a long lifespan, often living between 12 to 15 years or more when properly cared for.

The Cavapoo's popularity has led to the establishment of breed-specific rescue organizations that focus on finding homes for Cavapoos in need, offering a second chance to these wonderful dogs.

Cavapoochon

History of the Cavapoochon

The Cavapoochon is a charming and relatively new hybrid breed that has gained popularity among dog lovers in recent years. It is a crossbreed between a Cavalier King Charles Spaniel, a Poodle, and a Bichon Frise. While the exact origins of the Cavapoochon are not well-documented, it is believed to have emerged in the early 2000s as part of the growing trend of creating designer dog breeds.

The breeding of the Cavapoochon aimed to combine the desirable traits of its parent breeds. The Cavalier King Charles Spaniel is known for its affectionate nature and gentle temperament, while Poodles and Bichon Frises are intelligent and hypoallergenic. The goal was to create a small, friendly, and hypoallergenic dog that would make an excellent companion for individuals and families alike.

What is Unique about the Cavapoochon

The Cavapoochon is a delightful blend of the Cavalier King Charles Spaniel, Poodle, and Bichon Frise, making it a breed that stands out in the canine world. One of the first things that captures one's attention is their heart-melting appearance. With the irresistible facial features reminiscent of the Cavalier King Charles Spaniel, combined with the curly or wavy, low-shedding coat typical of both the Poodle and Bichon Frise, they are the epitome of canine cuteness. Their soft fur, expressive eyes, and diminutive size make them a favorite among dog enthusiasts. Furthermore, their hypoallergenic coat, a legacy from their Poodle and Bichon Frise lineage, means they shed minimally, providing relief for those sensitive to pet hair.

Cavapoochon / Bridgendboy / iStockphoto.com

But it's not just their looks that endear them to families. These dogs are blessed with a warm and friendly temperament, largely inherited from the Cavalier King Charles Spaniel. They are quick to form profound bonds with their human companions, consistently showcasing their affectionate and sociable nature. Additionally, the intelligence bestowed upon them by both the Poodle and Bichon Frise ensures they are sharp-witted and responsive. This makes training a joy, as the Cavapoochon is not only keen on mental challenges but is also eager to win the approval of their beloved owners.

Temperament and Personality of the Cavapoochon

Cavapoochons are the embodiment of warmth and charm, traits they effortlessly weave into the lives of their families. At the core of their nature lies an immense affection for humans. These canines have an innate need for human companionship, and this manifests in the deep bonds they create with their owners. Their heritage from the Cavalier King Charles Spaniel ensures they approach the world with an open heart, making them sociable and friendly not just to humans, but to other animals as well. Families can expect plenty of joyful moments, as these dogs are the epitome of playfulness, constantly seeking interactive games and fun activities to indulge in. But it's not all play; their Poodle and Bichon Frise lineage bestows upon them a commendable intelligence, making them astute learners who can master commands and tricks rapidly. Moreover, the Cavapoochon's adaptable nature is a testament to their versatility. Whether in a cozy apartment or a sprawling residence, they find ways to fit in seamlessly, proving that their main requirement is a loving environment complemented by sufficient attention and exercise.

Care for the Cavapoochon

To keep your Cavapoochon healthy and happy, it's important to provide proper care in terms of feeding, exercise, grooming, and monitoring their overall health. Here are some essential care guidelines:

1. Feeding: Provide your Cavapoochon with a well-balanced, high-

quality dog food that suits their age, size, and activity level. Consult with your veterinarian to determine the appropriate portion sizes and feeding schedule for your dog.
2. Exercise: While Cavapoochons are small dogs, they still need regular exercise to maintain their physical and mental well-being. Daily walks, playtime, and interactive toys can help meet their exercise needs. Aim for at least 30 minutes to an hour of exercise each day.
3. Grooming: The grooming needs of Cavapoochons can vary depending on their coat type. If your Cavapoochon has a curly or wavy coat, regular brushing is necessary to prevent matting and tangles. Some owners prefer to keep their Cavapoochons' coat shorter for easier maintenance. Additionally, regular dental care, ear cleaning, and nail trimming are important parts of their grooming routine.
4. Health Problems: Like any breed, Cavapoochons can be prone to certain health issues. Some common health concerns include heart problems, eye conditions, allergies, and joint issues. Regular veterinary check-ups, a balanced diet, regular exercise, and maintaining a healthy weight can help minimize the risk of these problems. It's important to be aware of potential breed-specific health concerns and discuss them with your veterinarian.

Training the Cavapoochon

Training a Cavapoochon often feels less like a chore and more like a rewarding journey, all thanks to their innate intelligence and fervent desire to make their owners happy. The cornerstone of any successful training endeavor with this breed lies in positive reinforcement. As you embark on this training journey, arm yourself with treats, heartfelt praise, and engaging play sessions. These act as potent motivators, inspiring your Cavapoochon to adhere to good behavior and excel in learning tasks. It's imperative, however, to steer clear of any harsh training measures. Such techniques not only prove ineffective but also jeopardize the treasured bond you share with your pet. The world is a vast playground for these young pups, and the sooner they get to explore it, the better. Early socialization, filled with diverse and positive experiences, can shape a Cavapoochon's demeanor, fostering confidence and minimizing any tendencies toward fear or aggression. Consistency acts as the backbone of effective training. Establishing clear expectations and adhering to them ensures that your Cavapoochon can navigate their learning curve with clarity. And while patience will be your greatest ally, remember to lay the groundwork with essential commands. Basics like 'sit', 'stay', and 'come' don't just instill discipline but also ensure your furry companion remains safe and sound in varying circumstances.

Benefits of the Cavapoochon

Owning a Cavapoochon can bring numerous benefits to your life. Here are some advantages of this delightful breed:

1. Hypoallergenic: Many Cavapoochons have a low-shedding and hypoallergenic coat, making them suitable for individuals with allergies or sensitivities to pet hair.
2. Companion and Family Dog: Cavapoochons are known for their friendly and affectionate nature, making them excellent companions and family dogs. They often get along well with children and other pets, forming strong bonds within the family unit.
3. Intelligence and Trainability: With their Poodle and Bichon Frise heritage, Cavapoochons are intelligent and trainable. They are

quick learners and can excel in obedience training, tricks, and various canine activities.
4. Adaptable Size: Cavapoochons come in various sizes, depending on the parental lines and the generations involved in the crossbreeding.

Interesting Facts about the Cavapoochon

1. Triple Breed Mix: The Cavapoochon is a delightful blend of three distinct breeds: the Cavalier King Charles Spaniel, the Bichon Frise, and the Poodle. This unique combination gives them a distinctive appearance and temperament.
2. Forever Puppy" Appearance: One of the most endearing qualities of the Cavapoochon is its perpetual puppy-like appearance. Even as they grow older, they often retain a youthful look, earning them the nickname "forever puppy."
3. Low Shedding: Thanks to their Poodle and Bichon Frise heritage, Cavapoochons often possess a coat that sheds minimally, making them an attractive option for individuals sensitive to pet hair.
4. Long Lifespan: With proper care, a Cavapoochon can have a relatively long lifespan, often ranging between 12 to 16 years or more.
5. Color Variations: The coat of a Cavapoochon can come in various colors, including cream, gold, white, tan, and even multi-colored patterns.
6. Adaptable Companions: Cavapoochons are known for their adaptability. Whether living in an apartment in the city or a home in the countryside, they can adjust well as long as they receive adequate love and care.
7. Health Vigilance: Due to their mixed breed nature, Cavapoochons can inherit health concerns from any of their three parent breeds.

Regular veterinary check-ups are essential to ensure they remain healthy.
8. Eager to Please: Their friendly and affectionate nature often makes them eager to please their owners, which can be an advantage during training sessions.
9. Great Therapy Dogs: Owing to their gentle and loving disposition, Cavapoochons are often considered excellent candidates for therapy and emotional support roles.
10. Family-Friendly: Their sociable and gentle nature makes them particularly well-suited for families. They tend to form close bonds with children and can get along well with other pets.

The Cavapoochon, with its unique heritage and endearing qualities, is undoubtedly a breed that captivates the hearts of many dog enthusiasts.

Cockapoo

History of the Cockapoo

The Cockapoo is a popular hybrid breed that combines the traits of a Cocker Spaniel and a Poodle. The breed's origin can be traced back to the United States in the mid-20th century when breeders began intentionally crossing these two breeds to create a new type of companion dog. The goal was to combine the Cocker Spaniel's friendly nature and appealing looks with the Poodle's intelligence and low-shedding coat.

The Cockapoo is considered one of the first designer dog breeds, and its popularity quickly grew due to its desirable qualities. The breed's development aimed to produce a dog that retained the positive attributes of both parent breeds while minimizing potential health issues often associated with purebred dogs.

What is Unique about the Cockapoo

The Cockapoo, with its blend of Cocker Spaniel and Poodle lineage, is cherished for its distinctive and often unpredictable appearance. Their coat, a defining feature, can vary greatly from one dog to the next. It can manifest as straight, wavy, or curly, and feel anywhere from silky and soft to dense or even wiry. Such variety stems from the specific genetic contributions of its parent breeds.

Cockapoo / Hugo Kruip / Unsplash.com

In addition to their versatile aesthetic, Cockapoos possess a notable advantage for many households: their potential hypoallergenic qualities. Owing to their Poodle genes, a significant number of Cockapoos boast a coat that sheds little to none, making them an excellent companion for allergy sufferers or those keen on minimal pet grooming. Furthermore, these delightful dogs aren't one-size-fits-all. Depending on the size of the Poodle in their ancestry, Cockapoos can range from the petite toy variety to the more robust standard size, allowing families and individuals to select a pet that perfectly fits their lifestyle and living space.

Temperament and Personality of the Cockapoo

The Cockapoo is renowned for its affectionate and engaging disposition. At the heart of this breed is its deep-rooted affection towards its human companions. Cockapoos are not just pets; they are family members, seamlessly integrating into daily life, always eager to participate in family activities. Their friendly demeanor isn't limited to their human family alone. Known for their sociable nature, Cockapoos exhibit a warmth that extends to other animals and people, especially children. Their gentleness and tolerance make them an excellent choice for households with kids. But it's not just their amiable nature that endears them to families; their intelligence is another commendable trait. Drawing from the astute Poodle and the ever-eager-to-please Cocker Spaniel, Cockapoos are often quick on the uptake, making training sessions a breeze when positive reinforcement techniques are employed. However, potential owners shouldn't mistake their amiability for lethargy. Cockapoos, vibrant in spirit, need their daily dose of exercise, be it walks, play sessions, or other stimulating activities, to keep them at their happiest and healthiest.

Care for the Cockapoo

1. **Feeding:** Providing a well-balanced diet that meets the specific nutritional needs of Cockapoos is essential. The amount and type of food may vary depending on the dog's age, size, activity level, and overall health. Consult with a veterinarian to determine the best diet plan for your Cockapoo.
2. **Exercise:** Cockapoos need regular exercise to maintain their physical and mental well-being. Daily walks, interactive play sessions, and mental stimulation activities are important to prevent boredom and keep them happy.
3. **Grooming:** The grooming requirements of Cockapoos depend on their coat type. Regular brushing is necessary to prevent matting and tangling, especially for dogs with longer and curlier coats. Cockapoos may require professional grooming every few months to maintain a neat appearance.
4. **Health Problems:** While Cockapoos are generally healthy dogs, they can be prone to certain health issues inherited from their parent breeds. Some common health concerns include ear infections, dental problems, luxating patella, and eye conditions. Regular vet check-ups, a balanced diet, exercise, and proper grooming can help minimize the risk of these problems.

Training the Cockapoo

Training a Cockapoo offers a rewarding experience, both for the dog and the owner, given the breed's intelligence and eagerness to please. To ensure success, the foundation of training should be built on consistency. Establishing regular routines and sticking to set rules helps the Cockapoo grasp expectations more rapidly. Equally important is the emphasis on positive reinforcement. A treat, a word of praise, or a brief play session can go a long way in motivating these delightful canines. They thrive on positive feedback, making them responsive to reward-based training. Alongside this, the importance of early socialization cannot be overstated. Introducing your Cockapoo to diverse settings, people, and other animals fosters confidence and curtails the development of undesirable behaviors. Furthermore, basic obedience training is paramount. While teaching commands like "sit," "stay," and "come" equips them for day-to-day life, considering structured puppy or obedience classes can further enhance their skills and deepen the bond shared between pet and owner. With commitment and understanding, training a Cockapoo promises a harmonious and fulfilling companionship.

Benefits of the Cockapoo

1. **Hypoallergenic Qualities:** Many Cockapoos have a low-shedding or hypoallergenic coat, making them suitable for individuals with allergies or those who prefer a cleaner home environment.
2. **Friendly and Social:** Cockapoos are known for their friendly and sociable nature, making them great companions for families, including children and other pets.
3. **Intelligence and Trainability:** With the combination of the Poodle's intelligence and the Cocker Spaniel's willingness to please, Cockapoos are highly trainable and excel in various training activities.
4. **Versatility:** Cockapoos come in different sizes, allowing potential owners to choose a size that fits their lifestyle and living arrangements.

Interesting Facts about the Cockapoo

1. Cockapoos are often referred to as "designer dogs" or "hybrid dogs" because they are the result of intentionally crossbreeding two purebred dog breeds.
2. The Cockapoo's appearance can vary widely within the same litter due to the genetic influence from both parent breeds.
3. Cockapoos have gained popularity due to their hypoallergenic coat, making them an attractive choice for individuals who typically experience allergies around dogs.
4. The breed's name, Cockapoo, is a combination of "Cocker" from Cocker Spaniel and "Poo" from Poodle.
5. Cockapoos are known for their friendly and affectionate nature, making them excellent therapy dogs and emotional support animals.
6. Some Cockapoos inherit the Poodle's intelligence and the Cocker Spaniel's hunting instincts, making them adept at various canine sports and activities.
7. Cockapoos are generally adaptable dogs that can thrive in both city and rural environments, as long as their exercise and socialization needs are met.
8. The popularity of Cockapoos has led to the establishment of breed-specific rescue organizations dedicated to finding homes for Cockapoos in need.

Cockapoochon

History of the Cockapoochon

The Cockapoochon is a delightful hybrid breed that has gained popularity in recent years. It is a cross between a Cockapoo (a mix of Cocker Spaniel and Poodle) and a Bichon Frise. While the exact origins of the Cockapoochon are unclear, it is believed to have emerged as part of the designer dog trend in the United States during the early 2000s.

The Cockapoochon was developed with the aim of combining the desirable traits of both parent breeds. Cockapoos are known for their friendly and affectionate nature, while Bichon Frises are cheerful and sociable. The goal was to create a small to medium-sized dog that possessed the Cockapoo's intelligence, adaptability, and low-shedding coat, along with the Bichon Frise's playful and people-oriented personality.

What is Unique about the Cockapoochon

The Cockapoochon stands out due to its charming and distinctive appearance. It inherits the curly or wavy, low-shedding coat from the Poodle side of its lineage, which makes it an excellent choice for individuals with allergies. The coat of the Bichon Frise parent adds an extra touch of softness and fluffiness to the mix. The Cockapoochon's coat can come in a variety of colors, including white, cream, apricot, chocolate, or a combination of these hues, contributing to its uniqueness and visual appeal.

In addition to its coat, the Cockapoochon also possesses a delightful blend of personality traits from both parent breeds. This breed tends to be friendly, loving, and eager to please, making it an excellent companion for individuals and families alike. The Cockapoochon's playful and sociable nature makes it well-suited for households with children and other pets.

Temperament and Personality of the Cockapoochon

Cockapoochons are known for their delightful temperament and lovable personality. They are often described as being affectionate, intelligent, and lively. With the combination of their Cocker Spaniel, Poodle, and Bichon Frise heritage, they tend to be sociable and enjoy being around people and other animals. Cockapoochons are often quick learners, making them adaptable to various training activities and commands.

This breed is well-suited for individuals or families seeking a devoted and loving companion. Cockapoochons thrive on human interaction and enjoy being part of the family. They are generally good-natured and often exhibit a gentle and patient demeanor, which makes them excellent therapy dogs or emotional support animals.

Care for the Cockapoochon

1. Feeding: Cockapoochons require a well-balanced diet to maintain their health. It is important to provide them with high-quality dog food that meets their nutritional needs. The specific feeding requirements may vary based on the size, age, and activity level of the individual dog. Consult with a veterinarian to determine the best feeding regimen for your Cockapoochon.
2. Exercise: Cockapoochons are energetic dogs and require regular exercise to keep them physically and mentally stimulated. Daily walks, interactive play sessions, and opportunities for socialization are essential to meet their exercise needs. These activities help prevent boredom and ensure that your Cockapoochon remains happy and healthy.
3. Grooming: The grooming needs of Cockapoochons will depend on the type of coat they inherit. If they have a curly or wavy coat, regular brushing is necessary to prevent matting and keep their fur tangle-free. Additionally, professional grooming may be required every few months to maintain a well-groomed appearance. It is important to pay attention to the Cockapoochon's ears, as they are prone to ear infections due to their floppy ear structure.
4. Health Problems: Cockapoochons, like any other breed, can be prone to certain health issues. Some common health concerns may include ear infections, dental problems, allergies, and progressive retinal atrophy (PRA). Regular visits to the veterinarian, a balanced diet, and maintaining good dental hygiene can help minimize the risk of these problems. Additionally, regular grooming and cleaning of the ears can help prevent ear infections.

Training the Cockapoochon

Training a Cockapoochon should start early and focus on positive reinforcement techniques. They are intelligent dogs and generally respond well to reward-based training methods. Early socialization is crucial to help them become well-rounded and confident dogs. Consistency, patience, and using positive reinforcement techniques such as treats, praise, and playtime will yield the best results. Cockapoochons are eager to please, so training sessions should be kept interesting and engaging to maintain their attention and motivation.

Benefits of the Cockapoochon

The Cockapoochon offers several benefits to potential owners:

1. Adaptable Size: Cockapoochons come in various sizes, ranging from small to medium, which allows potential owners to choose a size that fits their lifestyle and living arrangements.
2. Affectionate and Social: Cockapoochons are known for their loving and sociable nature, making them excellent companions for individuals, families, and households with other pets.
3. Low-Shedding Coat: Many Cockapoochons have a low-shedding coat, inherited from their Poodle and Bichon Frise parents, which makes them a great choice for individuals with allergies or those who prefer a low-maintenance coat.
4. Intelligence and Trainability: With their Cocker Spaniel, Poodle, and Bichon Frise heritage, Cockapoochons are intelligent and trainable, making them suitable for various training activities and commands.

Interesting Facts about the Cockapoochon

1. The Cockapoochon's name is a combination of "Cockapoo," referring to the Cocker Spaniel and Poodle mix, and "Bichon," representing the Bichon Frise.
2. The Cockapoochon's coat can vary in texture, ranging from wavy to curly, depending on the combination of its parent breeds.
3. Cockapoochons are often considered to be hypoallergenic or low-allergy dogs due to their low-shedding coat, but individual allergies may still vary.
4. This breed is known for its happy and playful disposition, bringing joy and entertainment to its family.
5. Cockapoochons can be highly adaptable and thrive in various living environments, including apartments or houses with yards.
6. Like their parent breeds, Cockapoochons are often sought after as therapy dogs due to their gentle and patient nature.
7. Cockapoochons enjoy human companionship and may experience separation anxiety if left alone for extended periods. They are best suited for households where someone is available to spend time with them.

The Cockapoochon is an endearing and lovable breed that combines the best qualities of the Cockapoo and the Bichon Frise. With their charming personalities, intelligence, and low-shedding coat, Cockapoochons make wonderful companions for a variety of individuals and families seeking a devoted and affectionate pet.

Corgipoo

History of the Corgipoo

The Corgipoo is a delightful hybrid breed that combines the Pembroke Welsh Corgi and the Poodle. While the exact origins of the Corgipoo are uncertain, it is believed to have emerged in the early 2000s, alongside the rise in popularity of designer dog breeds. Breeders aimed to create a companion dog that would inherit the charming looks of the Corgi and the desirable traits of the Poodle.

The Pembroke Welsh Corgi, known for its short legs, long body, and expressive face, has a rich history as a herding dog in Wales. On the other hand, the Poodle, available in various sizes, is renowned for its intelligence, versatility, and hypoallergenic coat. Combining these two breeds resulted in a unique and lovable companion: the Corgipoo.

What is Unique about the Corgipoo

The Corgipoo, with its distinctive appearance and delightful temperament, is a breed that captures the heart. At first glance, one can't help but be drawn to its unique physical attributes, a blend of the Corgi's endearing short legs and long body combined with the Poodle's curly or wavy coat. This fusion not only ensures a diverse palette of coat colors, ranging from tan and sable to black and white, but also a delightful juxtaposition of form that adds to its appeal. Dive deeper into understanding the breed, and the Corgipoo's temperament further stands out. It amalgamates the Corgi's friendliness and affection with the Poodle's intelligence and zest for life, resulting in a lively companion that thrives on human interaction. This breed's adaptability is another commendable trait; it's comfortable in both spacious homes with sprawling gardens or the confines of city apartments. However, their adaptability doesn't negate their need for activity; ensuring they're mentally and physically engaged is paramount. Furthermore, training a Corgipoo is relatively straightforward given their intelligence and eagerness to please. A combination of early socialization, consistent routines, and positive reinforcement will yield a companion that's not just well-behaved, but also a joyful addition to any household.

Corgipoo

Temperament and Personality of the Corgipoo

The Corgipoo breed radiates warmth and charm in spades thanks to its harmonic combination of Corgi and Poodle characteristics. The Corgipoo's lovable nature stands out as a distinguishing quality that appeals to both families and individuals. These dogs become more than just pets; they are valued friends because they frequently show their families deep devotion. They don't sacrifice intelligence for their love of company. Corgipoos are sharp-witted, vivacious, and always ready for a mind-bending puzzle toy or an interactive game, ensuring they keep their owners on their toes. They also have a hint of the Poodle's legendary intellect. Their outgoing disposition extends beyond their close relatives. Corgipoos are a great choice for families looking for an inclusive pet that enjoys participating in family events because they get along great with kids and other animals when they are properly socialized. Their friendly demeanor does not, however, imply that they are not vigilant. Because of their Corgi lineage, Corgipoos are frequently vigilant and protective. Despite their lack of hostility, they make excellent watchdogs who are always prepared to warn their family if anything is amiss because to their strong senses and protective instincts.

Care for the Corgipoo

Caring for a Corgipoo involves attention to their dietary needs, exercise requirements, grooming routines, and potential health issues. Here are some important considerations:

1. Feeding: Provide your Corgipoo with a balanced and high-quality diet that suits their age, size, and activity level. Consult with a veterinarian to determine the appropriate portion sizes and

nutritional requirements.
2. Exercise: While Corgipoos are not as high-energy as some other breeds, they still require regular exercise to maintain their overall health and prevent weight gain. Daily walks, playtime, and mental stimulation through interactive toys or training activities are beneficial.
3. Grooming: The grooming needs of a Corgipoo may vary based on the type of coat they inherit. If they have a wavy or curly coat, regular brushing is necessary to prevent matting and keep their fur in good condition. Occasional professional grooming may be required to maintain a neat appearance.
4. Health Problems: Like any breed, Corgipoos may be prone to certain health issues, although crossbreeding can potentially reduce the risk of inheriting breed-specific problems. Some potential health concerns to be aware of include hip dysplasia, patellar luxation, progressive retinal atrophy (PRA), and certain skin allergies. Regular veterinary check-ups, a balanced diet, and maintaining a healthy lifestyle can help minimize these risks.

Training the Corgipoo

Embarking on the journey of training a Corgipoo is both rewarding and engaging, especially given their intrinsic intelligence and their natural inclination to please their owners. Initiating this training journey early, ideally when they're still puppies, sets the stage for a lifelong bond between the dog and the owner. It provides an opportunity for the Corgipoo to grasp the fundamentals, from simple commands to adapting confidently to diverse environments. The key to unlocking their full potential is positive reinforcement. Showering them with treats, praise, and play when they exhibit the desired behavior not only bolsters their confidence but also strengthens their trust in their human counterpart. However, every training journey is dotted with challenges, and with Corgipoos, it's their occasional stubbornness. Overcoming this requires a blend of patience and unwavering consistency. It's crucial to establish clear boundaries and to be persistent in enforcing them. Yet, the essence of training isn't confined to commands alone. Socialization plays a pivotal role in molding a Corgipoo's character. Regular exposure to varied environments, people, and other animals ensures they grow up to be confident and amiable, minimizing tendencies toward fear or undue aggression.

Benefits of the Corgipoo

Owning a Corgipoo can bring numerous advantages and joys to your life:

1. Lovable Companion: Corgipoos are known for their affectionate and loyal nature. They often form strong bonds with their owners and become devoted family companions.
2. Family-Friendly: Corgipoos are generally good with children, making them suitable for families. Their playful and sociable temperament allows them to interact well with kids of different ages.
3. Moderate Exercise Needs: While they still require daily exercise, Corgipoos have moderate activity requirements compared to some higher-energy breeds. This makes them suitable for individuals or families who can provide regular exercise but may not have an extremely active lifestyle.
4. Intelligence and Trainability: Corgipoos inherit the intelligence of both the Corgi and Poodle, making them trainable and quick learners. Their willingness to please and ability to pick up commands makes them versatile and suitable for various training

activities.

Interesting Facts about the Corgipoo

1. Corgipoos are often referred to as "Corgi Doodles" due to their Poodle ancestry and the popular trend of doodle hybrid breeds.
2. The size of a Corgipoo can vary depending on the size of the Poodle used in the breeding process. Miniature Poodles will produce smaller Corgipoos, while Standard Poodles can result in larger ones.
3. Corgipoos are often sought after for their hypoallergenic coat, which can be more compatible with individuals who typically experience allergies around dogs.
4. Due to their intelligence and calm demeanor, some Corgipoos excel as therapy dogs, providing comfort and support to those in need.
5. Corgipoos may inherit the herding instinct of the Corgi, which can manifest as nipping or chasing behaviors. Proper training and redirection techniques can help manage these instincts effectively.
6. While Corgipoos are a popular designer breed, it's important to note that they are not recognized as a distinct breed by major kennel clubs, such as the American Kennel Club (AKC) or the Kennel Club (UK).

These fascinating facts and the unique characteristics of the Corgipoo make them an appealing choice for dog lovers seeking a loving and intelligent companion.

Danoodle

History of the Danoodle

The Danoodle is a unique and intriguing hybrid breed that combines the qualities of a Great Dane and a Poodle. While the exact origins of the Danoodle are not well-documented, it is believed to have emerged during the rise of designer dog breeds, which began in the late 20th century. The purpose of breeding Danoodles was to create a dog that possesses the Poodle's intelligence and hypoallergenic coat, along with the Great Dane's regal appearance and gentle temperament.

The breeding of Danoodles involves crossing a purebred Great Dane with a purebred Poodle, typically a Standard Poodle or a Miniature Poodle. The intention is to produce a dog that embodies the best characteristics of both parent breeds. The Great Dane is known for its imposing size, elegance, and calm demeanor, while the Poodle brings intelligence, trainability, and a non-shedding coat to the mix. The result is a breed that combines the nobility and grace of the Great Dane with the Poodle's versatility and intelligence.

FROM POODLES TO DOODLES

Danoodle / Erik Mclean / Pexels.com

What is Unique about the Danoodle

The Danoodle, a captivating blend of the Great Dane and the Poodle, offers a unique fusion of size and coat variations that make it a standout choice for dog enthusiasts. One of the most remarkable features of the Danoodle is its versatile size. While some Danoodles boast the imposing stature reminiscent of the Great Dane, others lean towards a more compact frame if bred from a Miniature Poodle. This variability allows potential pet owners the luxury of choosing a dog that aligns with their living conditions and size preferences.

Equally enchanting is the breed's diverse coat characteristics. The luxurious coat of a Danoodle might exhibit the curly or wavy finesse of a Poodle, or it could mimic the sleek, short texture of the Great Dane. There are also instances where these dogs brandish a delightful blend of both coat styles. Not to mention, their coats are a canvas of multiple colors, ranging from solid hues to fascinating mixtures of different shades. And, for those who are allergy-prone, the Danoodle presents a breath of fresh air. Thanks to the Poodle lineage, many Danoodles possess a hypoallergenic coat that curbs the amount of allergens released into the environment, making life a tad easier for allergy sufferers.

But what truly endears the Danoodle to families and individuals is its temperament. Often embodying the serene and dignified demeanor of the Great Dane, Danoodles are typically friendly, sociable, and astonishingly gentle, considering their size. These gentle giants wear their hearts on their sleeves, gracefully interacting with children, other pets, and even serving as empathetic therapy dogs. Their majestic presence, combined with their amiable nature, cements their position as an ideal choice for many families.

Temperament and Personality of the Danoodle

The Danoodle, a wonderful cross between the Great Dane and the Poodle, is praised for both its adorable personality and its distinctive appearance. A gentle and everlasting loyalty that is at the core of its character is something that it prominently inherited from the Great Dane. These dogs are a picture of patience and have an unmatched love for their families, creating ties that will last a lifetime.

Due to the Poodle genes running through it, this breed also has an exceptional level of intelligence. They are extremely trainable and thrive in circumstances with ongoing mental difficulties thanks to their keen intellect and desire to please. They speak in terms of positive reinforcement and joyfully accept treats, compliments, and moderate correction. Danoodles are charming in social situations and easily get along with both people and other animals. Particularly noteworthy are their propensity for children and capacity to adjust to families with several pets. They have a friendly aura, yet they also have a relaxing aura. Danoodles emit a calm and relaxing atmosphere, in contrast to some breeds that are bustling with energy, making them the perfect canine friend for individuals looking for peace and quiet.

Care for the Danoodle

To ensure the health and well-being of your Danoodle, it's essential to provide proper care in terms of feeding, exercise, grooming, and monitoring their health. Here are some care guidelines:

1. Feeding: Danoodles require a balanced diet appropriate for their size, age, and activity level. High-quality dog food that meets their nutritional needs, such as premium dry kibble or wet food,

is recommended. Consult with a veterinarian to determine the appropriate portion sizes and feeding schedule.
2. Exercise: While the Danoodle is not as energetic as some other breeds, regular exercise is still necessary to keep them physically and mentally stimulated. Daily walks, play sessions, and opportunities for socialization are essential. Aim for at least 30 minutes to an hour of exercise each day, depending on your Danoodle's size and energy levels.
3. Grooming: The grooming requirements of a Danoodle depend on the type of coat it inherits. If it has a curly or wavy coat, regular brushing is necessary to prevent matting and keep the fur free of tangles. Additionally, professional grooming may be required every few months to maintain a well-groomed appearance. It's important to clean the ears regularly, trim the nails when needed, and brush their teeth to ensure overall hygiene.
4. Health Problems: Like all dog breeds, Danoodles can be prone to certain health issues. While hybrid vigor can help reduce the risk of inheriting some genetic problems, it's essential to be aware of potential health concerns. These may include hip dysplasia, bloat, eye diseases, and cardiac issues. Regular veterinary check-ups, a balanced diet, exercise, and a healthy lifestyle can help minimize the risk of these problems. It is advisable to work with a reputable breeder who conducts health screenings on their breeding dogs to reduce the chances of hereditary issues.

Training the Danoodle

Training a Danoodle is a rewarding journey that ideally commences in their early, formative stages. With their innate intelligence and eagerness to please, these crossbreeds are generally amenable to training, but the approach used is of paramount importance. At the heart of a successful Danoodle training regimen is positive reinforcement. Showering them with treats, praise, and various rewards when they exhibit desired behaviors not only facilitates quicker learning but also fosters trust and a stronger bond between the dog and owner. Given the Danoodle's sensitive nature, it's essential to steer clear of any punitive methods that could dampen their spirit or hinder their learning.

The world is a vast and varied place, and for a young Danoodle, early exposure to its diversity is crucial. By introducing them to a range of environments, individuals, other animals, and situations, they learn adaptability and cultivate a well-balanced demeanor. Alongside this broad socialization, fundamental obedience training is a must. Harnessing their innate intelligence, owners should instill foundational commands like sit, stay, and come. Furthermore, considering their size and potential strength, mastering leash walking early on is a must. For an enhanced structured learning environment, enrolling them in puppy classes or obedience training sessions can be incredibly beneficial, rounding out their education and further honing their sociable nature.

Benefits of the Danoodle

The Danoodle offers several benefits to potential owners:

1. Hypoallergenic Qualities: Many Danoodles have a low-shedding and hypoallergenic coat, making them a suitable choice for individuals with allergies or sensitivities to dog dander.
2. Family-Friendly: Danoodles are generally friendly and gentle with children and other pets, making them excellent family companions. Their calm demeanor and loyalty make them well-suited for households with multiple family members.
3. Intelligence and Trainability: With their Poodle heritage, Danoodles are intelligent and trainable. They excel in various training

activities, making them versatile companions for tasks such as therapy work, obedience competitions, and interactive games.
4. Size Variations: The Danoodle comes in different sizes, depending on the size of the Poodle parent used in the breeding process. This size variety allows potential owners to select a Danoodle that suits their living arrangements and lifestyle preferences.

Interesting Facts about the Danoodle

1. The name "Danoodle" is a combination of "Great Dane" and "Poodle," reflecting the parent breeds that make up this hybrid.
2. Danoodles can vary in size, with some individuals weighing as much as a Great Dane, while others may be smaller, similar to a Standard Poodle or Miniature Poodle.
3. The Danoodle's hypoallergenic coat has contributed to its popularity, as it provides an option for individuals who typically experience allergies around dogs.
4. Some Danoodles may inherit the Poodle's intelligence and the Great Dane's herding instincts, which can result in a dog that excels in various canine sports and activities.
5. Due to their size and calm demeanor, Danoodles can make excellent therapy dogs, providing comfort and support to those in need.
6. The first-generation Danoodles (F1) are the direct offspring of a Great Dane and a Poodle. Further breeding can result in multigenerational Danoodles (F2, F3, etc.), which can lead to more predictable traits and characteristics.
7. The popularity of Danoodles has led to the establishment of breed-specific rescue organizations dedicated to finding homes for Danoodles in need. Adoption can be a rewarding option for those interested in adding a Danoodle to their family while providing a

loving home for a dog in need.

By understanding the history, unique qualities, temperament, care requirements, training, benefits, and interesting facts about the Danoodle, you can gain a comprehensive understanding of this fascinating hybrid breed and provide the best care and companionship for your furry friend.

Doodleman

History of the Doodleman

The Doodleman is a unique hybrid breed that has gained popularity in recent years. It is a cross between a Doberman Pinscher and a Poodle, typically either a Standard Poodle or a Miniature Poodle. While the exact origins of the Doodleman are unclear, it is believed to have originated in the United States during the early 2000s as part of the designer dog trend.

The goal of breeding Doodleman was to combine the desirable traits of both parent breeds. Doberman Pinschers are known for their loyalty, intelligence, and protective nature, while Poodles are highly intelligent, hypoallergenic, and have a variety of coat types. The aim was to create a dog that possessed the Doberman Pinscher's loyalty and protective instinct along with the Poodle's intelligence and hypoallergenic qualities.

What is Unique about the Doodleman

The Doodleman stands out due to its unique combination of the Doberman Pinscher's sleek and athletic physique and the Poodle's variety of coat types. Depending on the specific cross, the Doodleman's coat can range from curly to wavy, and it may come in various colors, including black, brown, or white. This wide range of coat types and colors adds to the breed's visual appeal.

Another unique aspect of the Doodleman is its potential for hybrid vigor, which refers to the increased health and vitality often seen in crossbred animals. By combining the genetic diversity of the Doberman Pinscher and the Poodle, Doodleman breeders aim to produce dogs with improved overall health and reduced risk of breed-specific health issues.

Temperament and Personality of the Doodleman

Doodleman dogs are known for their loyal, intelligent, and protective nature. They are typically devoted to their families and have a strong desire to please their owners. Doodleman dogs often exhibit a high level of trainability and are quick learners, which makes them suitable for various training activities and tasks.

Due to their Doberman Pinscher heritage, Doodleman dogs can be naturally protective and may display guarding instincts. Early socialization and consistent, positive training are essential to ensure they develop into well-rounded and well-behaved dogs. Proper training and socialization can help them become friendly and accepting of strangers while still being vigilant watchdogs.

Doodleman dogs are generally good with children when properly socialized, although supervision is always recommended to ensure positive interactions. They can also get along well with other pets in the household when introduced and socialized appropriately from an early age.

Care for the Doodleman

1. **Feeding:** Doodleman dogs require a well-balanced diet to maintain their health. It is important to provide them with high-quality dog food that meets their nutritional needs. The specific feeding requirements may vary based on the size, age, and activity level of the individual dog. Consult with a veterinarian to determine the appropriate feeding regimen for your Doodleman.
2. **Exercise:** Doodleman dogs are energetic and require regular exercise to keep them physically and mentally stimulated. Daily walks, playtime, and interactive toys can help meet their exercise needs. Engaging them in activities that challenge their intelligence, such as puzzle toys or obedience training, can also help prevent boredom.
3. **Grooming:** The grooming needs of Doodleman dogs depend on the type of coat they inherit. If they have a curly or wavy coat, regular brushing is necessary to prevent matting and to keep their fur tangle-free. Professional grooming may be required every few months to maintain a well-groomed appearance. Additionally, regular dental care, nail trimming, and ear cleaning are essential parts of their overall grooming routine.
4. **Health Problems:** As with any dog breed, Doodleman dogs can be prone to certain health issues. While crossbreeding can help reduce the risk of some inherited conditions, they may still be susceptible to health problems seen in their parent breeds. It is important to work with a reputable breeder who conducts health screenings on their breeding dogs. Regular veterinary check-ups, a balanced diet, proper exercise, and maintaining a healthy lifestyle can help minimize the risk of potential health problems.

Training the Doodleman

Training a Doodleman should start early and focus on positive reinforcement techniques. They are intelligent dogs and generally respond well to reward-based training methods. Early socialization is crucial to help them become well-adjusted and confident dogs. Consistency, patience, and using positive reinforcement techniques such as treats, praise, and playtime will yield the best results.

Obedience training and basic commands should be a priority for Doodleman dogs due to their protective nature. Teaching them proper leash manners and ensuring they have a solid recall command is essential for their safety. As they are intelligent and eager to please, Doodleman dogs can excel in advanced training activities such as agility, obedience, or even specialized tasks like search and rescue.

Benefits of the Doodleman

The Doodleman offers several benefits to potential owners:

1. Loyalty and Protection: The Doodleman inherits the protective instincts of the Doberman Pinscher, making them loyal and excellent watchdogs. They can be vigilant and protective of their families, providing a sense of security.
2. Intelligence and Trainability: With their Poodle heritage, Doodleman dogs are intelligent and trainable. They thrive on mental stimulation and enjoy learning new commands and tasks, making them suitable for various training activities.
3. Hypoallergenic Qualities: Depending on the type of coat they inherit, many Doodleman dogs have low-shedding or hypoallergenic coats, making them a suitable choice for individuals with allergies or sensitivities to dog hair.

4. Versatility: Doodleman dogs can adapt well to different lifestyles and living arrangements. They can be active companions for individuals or families who enjoy outdoor activities, and they can also be content with regular exercise and mental stimulation in more urban environments.

Interesting Facts about the Doodleman

1. The Doodleman's name is a combination of "Doberman" and "Poodle," reflecting its parent breeds.
2. The size of Doodleman dogs can vary depending on the size of the Poodle used in the crossbreeding process. Miniature Poodles result in smaller Doodleman dogs, while Standard Poodles produce larger ones.
3. Doodleman dogs have gained popularity due to their potential for hypoallergenic coats, which makes them a suitable option for individuals who typically experience allergies around dogs.
4. Doodleman dogs are known for their alertness and natural protective instincts, which can make them excellent candidates for roles such as therapy dogs or working dogs.
5. Some Doodleman dogs inherit the Poodle's intelligence and Doberman Pinscher's athleticism, making them well-suited for various canine sports and activities.
6. The first-generation Doodleman (F1) is the direct offspring of a Doberman Pinscher and a Poodle. Further breeding can create multigenerational Doodleman dogs (F2, F3, etc.), which can lead to more predictable traits and appearances.

It is important to note that the Doodleman is a hybrid breed, and individual dogs may vary in their appearance, temperament, and other characteristics. Potential owners should always research and consult with reputable breeders to gain a better understanding of the specific traits and needs of the Doodleman breed.

Goldendoodle

History of the Goldendoodle

The Goldendoodle is a popular hybrid breed that combines the Golden Retriever and the Poodle. It emerged in the late 20th century as part of the designer dog trend, which sought to create new breeds by crossing two purebred dogs. The goal was to combine the desirable traits of the Golden Retriever, known for its friendly and gentle nature, with the Poodle, renowned for its intelligence and hypoallergenic coat.

The exact origins of the Goldendoodle are not well-documented, but it is believed to have originated in the United States in the 1990s. The breed was developed with the aim of creating a dog that possessed the Golden Retriever's friendly temperament and the Poodle's hypoallergenic qualities. Breeders hoped to produce a dog that would be suitable for individuals with allergies or asthma who still desired a dog with the traits of a Golden Retriever.

The Goldendoodle quickly gained popularity due to its appealing combination of traits. It became known for its friendly nature, intelligence, and low-shedding coat. Today, Goldendoodles are widely recognized and sought after as loving family pets and companion animals.

Goldendoodle / Graham Roy / Pexels.com

What is Unique about the Goldendoodle

The Goldendoodle boasts a plethora of captivating qualities that appeal to a wide range of potential owners. At first glance, one might be captivated by the Goldendoodle's stunning coat, which can manifest in an array of textures ranging from straight to wavy or even curly. This diversity not only caters to aesthetic preferences but also practical ones. Indeed, many Goldendoodles, owing to their Poodle lineage, possess hypoallergenic coats. Their reduced shedding and limited dander production make them particularly endearing to individuals who suffer from allergies or asthma.

Beyond their striking appearance, Goldendoodles are also treasures in terms of temperament and intelligence. Renowned for their sharp minds, they exhibit a zeal for learning and are exceptionally responsive to training. Whether it's simple commands, intricate tricks, or various dog sports, these dogs are keen to impress with their prowess. Pairing this intelligence with their naturally amiable disposition results in a dog that's both bright and affable. Their innate sociability extends to children, other pets, and even strangers, solidifying the Goldendoodle's reputation as an ideal family companion.

Temperament and Personality of the Goldendoodle

Goldendoodles have a reputation for being friendly, affectionate, and sociable dogs. And they are renowned for their warm and friendly disposition, a wonderful blend of the best attributes of their parent breeds. These dogs are notably gentle and loving, often forging deep connections with their families and cherishing the time they spend together. Their impressive intelligence, combined with an innate eagerness to please, makes them exceptionally trainable, frequently outshining others in obedience drills and various canine endeavors. Their affable nature extends to a broad spectrum of company, from children to other animals, underscoring their suitability as family pets. Alongside their sociable tendencies, Goldendoodles possess a playful and dynamic spirit, necessitating regular bouts of exercise to satisfy both their physical and intellectual appetites.

Care for the Goldendoodle

1. Feeding: Goldendoodles require a well-balanced diet that meets their nutritional needs. High-quality dog food, suitable for their size, age, and activity level, is recommended. Consult with a veterinarian to determine the appropriate feeding routine and portion sizes for your Goldendoodle.
2. Exercise: Goldendoodles are energetic dogs that require regular

exercise to keep them happy and healthy. Daily walks, playtime, and interactive activities are essential to meet their exercise needs. They also benefit from mental stimulation, such as puzzle toys and training sessions.
3. Grooming: The grooming needs of Goldendoodles can vary depending on their coat type. If they have a wavy or curly coat, regular brushing is necessary to prevent matting and tangling. Professional grooming may be required every few months to maintain a well-groomed appearance. It is also important to regularly clean their ears and trim their nails.
4. Health Problems: While Goldendoodles are generally healthy dogs, they can be prone to certain health issues inherited from their parent breeds. Common health concerns may include hip dysplasia, elbow dysplasia, progressive retinal atrophy (PRA), and certain genetic disorders. Regular vet check-ups, a balanced diet, appropriate exercise, and maintaining a healthy weight can help minimize the risk of these problems.

Training the Goldendoodle

Initiating training early is crucial for Goldendoodles; as soon as they step into their new homes, the foundation for their behavior and manners should be set. Early training not only shapes their conduct but also boosts their confidence, helping them evolve into well-adjusted dogs. These intelligent canines respond best to positive reinforcement, with treats, praise, and play acting as potent motivators. While their smarts are an advantage, consistency in training methods and an abundance of patience are key, especially when imparting basic commands like "sit," "stay," and "come." After they grasp the fundamentals, diving deeper into advanced training or specialized activities tailored to their unique skills and inclinations is beneficial.

Benefits of the Goldendoodle

The Goldendoodle offers several benefits to potential owners:

1. Hypoallergenic Qualities: Many Goldendoodles have a low-shedding and hypoallergenic coat, making them suitable for individuals with allergies or asthma.
2. Family-Friendly: Goldendoodles are typically friendly and gentle with children and other pets, making them excellent family companions.
3. Intelligence and Trainability: Goldendoodles inherit the intelligence of both parent breeds, making them trainable and suitable for various training activities and tasks.
4. Versatility: Goldendoodles come in different sizes, ranging from miniature to standard, allowing potential owners to choose a size that fits their lifestyle and living arrangements.

Interesting Facts about the Goldendoodle

1. The Goldendoodle's name is a combination of "Golden," referring to the Golden Retriever, and "Poodle."
2. Goldendoodles can come in a variety of coat colors, including shades of gold, cream, apricot, red, and black.
3. Some Goldendoodles inherit the Poodle's curly coat, while others have a wavy or straight coat. Curly-coated Goldendoodles are more likely to be hypoallergenic.
4. Goldendoodles have gained popularity as therapy and service dogs due to their intelligence, trainability, and friendly nature.
5. The size of Goldendoodles can vary depending on the size of the Poodle used in the crossbreeding process. Miniature Poodles result in smaller Goldendoodles, while Standard Poodles produce

larger ones.
6. Goldendoodles are social dogs and may experience separation anxiety if left alone for long periods. They thrive in homes where they receive plenty of attention and companionship.
7. The popularity of Goldendoodles has led to the establishment of breed-specific rescue organizations that specialize in finding homes for Goldendoodles in need.

Overall, the Goldendoodle is a lovable and intelligent hybrid breed that combines the best traits of the Golden Retriever and the Poodle. With their friendly nature, low-shedding coat, and trainability, they make wonderful companions for individuals and families alike.

Irish Doodle

History of the Irish Doodle

The Irish Doodle is a crossbreed that combines the traits of an Irish Setter and a Poodle. While the exact origin of the Irish Doodle is uncertain, it likely emerged in the United States as part of the designer dog trend. Breeders sought to create a hybrid that possessed the desirable characteristics of both parent breeds: the Irish Setter's elegant appearance and the Poodle's intelligence and hypoallergenic coat.

The Irish Setter is a breed with a rich history. It originated in Ireland during the 18th century and was primarily used as a hunting dog. The Irish Setter's distinctive red coat, friendly nature, and athleticism quickly made it popular as a companion and show dog. On the other hand, Poodles are known for their intelligence, versatility, and hypoallergenic qualities. By crossing these two breeds, breeders aimed to create a dog that combined the Irish Setter's beauty and the Poodle's desirable traits.

Irish Doodle / Pexels.com

What is Unique about the Irish Doodle

Irish Doodles possess distinctive characteristics that make them a breed of their own. Their coat, often wavy or curly like a Poodle's, is hypoallergenic and low-shedding, making them a favorite among allergy sufferers and those desiring minimal dog hair around the home. Their stunning array of coat colors, spanning from deep reds to gentle apricots and creams, contributes to their undeniable charm. Moreover, their size, which can vary from medium to large depending on the Poodle involved in the breeding, allows prospective owners flexibility in selecting a pet that best aligns with their living circumstances and preferences.

Temperament and Personality of the Irish Doodle

Irish Doodles are celebrated for their warm and engaging temperament. Their inherent playfulness and energy, inherited from the Irish Setter, ensures they thrive on regular physical activities, making them an ideal companion for those who enjoy outdoor adventures or playful interactions. Coupled with the intelligence and trainability from their Poodle lineage, these dogs are quick learners, eager to please, and respond remarkably well to positive reinforcement during training. Their deeply rooted family-oriented nature ensures that they form lasting bonds with their human companions, seamlessly integrating into family life and getting along wonderfully with children and other pets. Furthermore, with a touch of the Irish Setter's natural alertness, Irish Doodles often exhibit a protective instinct, ensuring their families feel both loved and safeguarded.

Care for the Irish Doodle

1. Feeding: Irish Doodles require a balanced diet that meets their nutritional needs. It is essential to provide them with high-quality dog food appropriate for their size, age, and activity level. Consult with a veterinarian for specific dietary recommendations.
2. Exercise: Irish Doodles are active dogs that need regular exercise to stay mentally and physically stimulated. Daily walks, playtime, and interactive activities are important to keep them happy and prevent behavioral issues.
3. Grooming: The grooming needs of Irish Doodles depend on the type of coat they inherit. Regular brushing is necessary to prevent matting and maintain a healthy coat. Occasional professional grooming may be required to keep their fur in good condition.
4. Health Problems: While hybrid vigor may reduce the risk of certain inherited health issues, Irish Doodles can still be prone to some of the conditions that affect their parent breeds. These may include hip dysplasia, progressive retinal atrophy (PRA), and certain genetic disorders. Regular veterinary check-ups, a healthy diet, and appropriate exercise can help maintain their overall well-being.

Training the Irish Doodle

After bringing a puppy home, Irish Doodle training should begin in its early stages. These clever dogs benefit from positive reinforcement tactics, which stress treats, affection, and vocal praise. Their intelligence and desire to please their masters allow them to learn commands quickly and enjoy fulfilling tasks. Dog and owner bonds typically strengthen during training, making these sessions enjoyable moments of connection and understanding. Beyond basic obedience training, early socializing is crucial to Irish Doodle growth. Early exposure to a variety of places, people, and animals shapes them into well-rounded people who handle varied situations with elegance and confidence. Proactive training builds a firm behavioral foundation and makes the Irish Doodle gregarious, versatile, and well-mannered.

Benefits of the Irish Doodle

Owning an Irish Doodle can provide several benefits:

1. Hypoallergenic Coat: Many Irish Doodles have a low-shedding and hypoallergenic coat, making them suitable for individuals with allergies or sensitivities to dog hair.
2. Companionship: Irish Doodles are known for their affectionate and friendly nature, making them excellent companions and family pets.
3. Intelligence and Trainability: With their Poodle lineage, Irish Doodles are intelligent and trainable, making them well-suited for various training activities and tasks.
4. Versatility: Irish Doodles come in different sizes, allowing individuals to choose a size that fits their preferences and living arrangements.

Interesting Facts about the Irish Doodle

1. Crossbreeding an Irish Setter with a Standard Poodle typically results in larger Irish Doodles, while using a Miniature or Toy Poodle can produce smaller-sized Irish Doodles.
2. Irish Doodles are often sought after for their hypoallergenic coats, which can be less likely to trigger allergies in some individuals.
3. Some Irish Doodles inherit the Irish Setter's love for water and

enjoy activities such as swimming.
4. Irish Doodles can excel in various canine sports and activities, thanks to their intelligence and athleticism.
5. The Irish Doodle's popularity has led to the establishment of breed-specific rescue organizations that focus on finding homes for Irish Doodles in need.
6. Irish Doodles are recognized for their beautiful, flowing coats and are often admired for their striking appearance.

Labradoodle

History of the Labradoodle

The Labradoodle is a popular poodle hybrid breed that originated in Australia in the 1980s. The breed was created by crossing a Labrador Retriever with a Standard Poodle. The original purpose of the Labradoodle was to combine the Labrador's friendly and trainable nature with the Poodle's hypoallergenic coat, making it suitable for individuals with allergies. The breed's development was primarily driven by Wally Conron, who was working as the breeding manager for the Royal Guide Dog Association of Australia at the time.

What is Unique about the Labradoodle

The Labradoodle is known for its unique coat, which can vary in texture and appearance. Labradoodles can have a variety of coat types, including straight, wavy, or curly hair. This diversity in coat texture makes it challenging to predict the exact coat type a Labradoodle will have, even within the same litter. Labradoodles can also come in a wide range of colors, including black, chocolate, cream, apricot, and silver.

Labradoodle Julissa Helmuth / Pexels.com

Temperament and Personality of the Labradoodle

Labradoodles are typically friendly, outgoing, and affectionate dogs. They are known for their intelligence, making them highly trainable and adaptable. Labradoodles often exhibit a high level of energy and enjoy being active and participating in various activities. They are generally good with children and other pets and tend to be social dogs that enjoy being part of a family. Labradoodles can also have a playful and mischievous side, keeping their owners entertained with their antics.

Care for the Labradoodle

1. Feeding: Labradoodles require a well-balanced diet that meets their nutritional needs. High-quality dog food, preferably formulated for medium to large breeds, is recommended. The specific feeding requirements may vary based on the dog's age, size, and activity level.
2. Exercise: Labradoodles are energetic dogs that require regular exercise to keep them physically and mentally stimulated. Daily walks and engaging activities such as retrieving or agility training can help meet their exercise needs. Labradoodles enjoy spending time outdoors and thrive in active households.
3. Grooming: The grooming needs of Labradoodles can vary depending on their coat type. Labradoodles with wavy or curly coats require regular brushing to prevent matting and tangling. They may also need professional grooming every few months to maintain a well-groomed appearance. Labradoodles with straighter coats may require less grooming but still benefit from regular brushing to remove loose hair.
4. Health Problems: Labradoodles can be prone to certain health

issues, similar to their parent breeds. Common health concerns in Labradoodles include hip dysplasia, elbow dysplasia, progressive retinal atrophy (PRA), and certain genetic disorders. Regular vet check-ups, a balanced diet, exercise, and maintaining a healthy weight can help minimize the risk of these problems.

Training the Labradoodle

Labradoodles are intelligent and eager to please, making them highly trainable. Positive reinforcement training methods, such as rewards, praise, and treats, work well with Labradoodles. They respond best to consistent and patient training techniques. Early socialization is crucial to help them develop good manners and become well-rounded dogs. Labradoodles thrive in training activities and can excel in obedience, agility, and even therapy work.

Benefits of the Labradoodle

The Labradoodle offers several benefits to potential owners:

1. Hypoallergenic: Labradoodles often inherit the Poodle's hypoallergenic coat, which produces less dander and is less likely to cause allergies in sensitive individuals.
2. Versatile: Labradoodles come in different sizes, ranging from miniature to standard, providing options for various living arrangements and lifestyles.
3. Family-Friendly: Labradoodles are typically gentle and good with children, making them excellent family pets.
4. Intelligence and Trainability: Labradoodles are intelligent dogs that are quick to learn and respond well to training. They can be taught various commands and tasks, making them suitable for

different training activities.
5. Companionship: Labradoodles form strong bonds with their families and thrive on human companionship. They are known for their affectionate and loyal nature.

Interesting Facts about the Labradoodle

1. The Labradoodle was initially bred to serve as a guide dog for individuals with allergies, combining the desirable traits of the Labrador Retriever and Poodle.
2. Labradoodles gained significant attention and popularity after being featured in media, including high-profile celebrities who owned Labradoodles as pets.
3. Labradoodles are often used as therapy dogs due to their friendly and gentle temperament, bringing comfort and joy to people in hospitals, nursing homes, and other care facilities.
4. Labradoodles can be found working in various service roles, including search and rescue, assistance dogs for people with disabilities, and as trained therapy dogs.
5. Some Labradoodles have successfully completed training to become skilled guide dogs for individuals with visual impairments.
6. Labradoodles have a strong retrieving instinct inherited from their Labrador Retriever parent. They enjoy playing fetch and participating in activities that involve retrieving objects.
7. Labradoodles have become so popular that they have their own dedicated breed clubs and organizations that promote responsible breeding and education about the breed.

The Labradoodle has captured the hearts of many dog lovers around the world, offering a delightful combination of intelligence, affection, and an allergy-friendly coat.

Maltipoo

History of the Maltipoo

The Maltipoo is a popular hybrid breed that is a cross between a Maltese and a Poodle. While the exact origin of the Maltipoo is uncertain, it is believed to have emerged in the United States during the late 20th century. The Maltipoo was created as a designer breed, combining the desirable traits of both parent breeds—the Maltese's charming personality and the Poodle's intelligence and hypoallergenic coat.

The purpose of breeding Maltipoos was to produce a small, affectionate companion dog with a low-shedding coat, suitable for individuals with allergies. The breed quickly gained popularity due to its adorable appearance and friendly temperament. Today, Maltipoos are cherished pets and continue to capture the hearts of dog lovers worldwide.

Maltipoo / Pexels.com

What is Unique about the Maltipoo

The Maltipoo has captivated the hearts of many dog enthusiasts with its blend of charm and practicality. Their aesthetic appeal is undeniable. With a coat that can oscillate between the Maltese's silky fluffiness and the Poodle's distinctive wavy texture, they parade a spectrum of colors from pristine white to rich apricot and shimmering silver. When combined with their soulful eyes and dainty noses, the result is a picture of endearing allure.

Beyond their looks, Maltipoos bring practical benefits to the table. Their hypoallergenic coat means they're the preferred choice for many allergy sufferers, as they tend to induce fewer reactions. Coupled with their modest size—typically weighing in at a manageable 5 to 15 pounds—they're ideal companions for city dwellers with limited space, or frequent travelers looking for a furry companion that's portable and adaptive.

However, what truly elevates the Maltipoo's standing in the canine community is its heartwarming demeanor and sharp intellect. These dogs are bundles of affection, often seeking the warmth of a lap or the joy of playful interactions with family members. Their sociability and loving nature make them a fitting addition to households of all configurations, from bustling families to solitary individuals. Furthermore, they carry a torch of intelligence passed down from both their parent breeds. This not only makes training sessions smoother but also calls for engaging activities that cater to their keen minds, turning playtime into an exciting blend of fun and mental workouts.

Temperament and Personality of the Maltipoo

With their appealing blend of vigor and loyalty, Maltipoos have won the hearts of dog lovers looking for a multifaceted companion. Their diminutive size betrays a vibrant vitality; these canines enjoy to play and participate in interactive activities. They are the perfect match for both busy people and families wishing to inject some lively fun into their everyday routines because of their love for life. They are extremely affectionate creatures, famed for the strong ties they form with their human counterparts, and it's not simply their playful personality that has won over so many. They become treasured family members rather than just pets because of their feeling of loyalty and intense desire to please.

They are friendly with people besides their primary caretakers. Maltipoos are renowned for their amiable and outgoing personalities. They frequently fit in with many pets in harmony and are sociable with strangers, especially when first met. Maltipoos are a great choice for families because they are nice and interesting playmates for kids in particular. But despite their kind nature, they are in no way weaklings. Maltipoos frequently act as effective watchdogs, alerting their owners to any unexpected sounds or potential threats. This shows that even the smallest canines can stand tall when it comes to guarding their loved ones. Maltipoos have quick hearing and a great sense of their surroundings.

Care for the Maltipoo

1. Feeding: Maltipoos should be fed a balanced diet of high-quality dog food suitable for their size, age, and activity level. The amount of food will depend on their individual needs, and it's important to monitor their weight to prevent obesity.

2. Exercise: While Maltipoos have moderate exercise requirements, they still need daily walks and playtime to stay mentally and physically stimulated. Interactive toys and games that challenge their intelligence can be beneficial.
3. Grooming: Maltipoos require regular grooming to maintain their coat's health and appearance. Brushing several times a week helps prevent matting and tangling. Professional grooming may be necessary every 6 to 8 weeks to keep their coat at an appropriate length.
4. Health Problems: Maltipoos, like all dog breeds, can be prone to certain health issues. Some common concerns include dental problems, eye conditions, allergies, and patellar luxation (kneecap dislocation). Regular veterinary check-ups, proper dental care, and a healthy lifestyle can help prevent or manage these conditions.

Training the Maltipoo

Training a Maltipoo is a rewarding endeavor that hinges on positive reinforcement techniques. By showering them with praise, treats, and rewards, these dogs are more receptive to learning. Starting their socialization early—by exposing them to a variety of people, animals, and environments—ensures they grow into well-adjusted and confident adults. Emphasizing basic commands like "sit", "stay", and "come" forms the foundation of their training, with consistency and patience being the key. Additionally, housetraining can be smoothly achieved with a structured approach, whether through crate training or assigning specific potty areas, always reinforced by positive feedback.

Benefits of the Maltipoo

Owning a Maltipoo can bring several advantages:

1. Hypoallergenic: Maltipoos' low-shedding coats make them a suitable option for individuals with allergies or sensitivities to pet dander.
2. Companion and Family Dog: Maltipoos thrive on companionship and make excellent family pets. Their friendly and gentle nature allows them to interact well with children and other pets.
3. Size Variety: Maltipoos come in different sizes, ranging from teacup to standard, providing options for various living situations and preferences.
4. Versatility: Maltipoos can adapt well to different environments, whether it's a cozy apartment or a spacious home. Their small size and low exercise requirements make them suitable for a range of lifestyles.

Interesting Facts about the Maltipoo

1. The Maltipoo's name is a combination of "Maltese" and "Poodle," signifying its parent breeds.
2. Maltipoos can have different coat types, including straight, wavy, or curly, depending on the combination of their parent's coat textures.
3. Some Maltipoos may have the tendency to bark more than others, but proper training and socialization can help manage their barking behavior.
4. Maltipoos are often used as therapy dogs due to their friendly and empathetic nature. They can provide comfort and emotional support to those in need.

5. The lifespan of a Maltipoo typically ranges from 10 to 15 years, although individual factors and care can influence their longevity.
6. Maltipoos enjoy being the center of attention and may become anxious or develop behavioral issues if left alone for long periods. They thrive in homes where they receive ample love and companionship.
7. Maltipoos are known for their intelligence and can excel in activities like agility, obedience, and trick training.

Newfypoo

History of the Newfypoo

The Newfypoo is a mix between a Poodle and a Newfoundland. The Newfypoo is thought to have originated in the United States in the late 20th century, however its precise origin is unknown. Similar to other poodle hybrids, the Newfypoo was created by breeders in an effort to blend the best qualities of both parent breeds.

The huge and docile breed known as a Newfoundland originated in Newfoundland, Canada, where fisherman employed them as working dogs to lift nets and save drowning victims. On the other hand, poodles are highly intelligent, adaptable, and available in a range of sizes and coat kinds. They are renowned for being trainable and hypoallergenic.

The goal of breeding Newfypoos was to produce a big, smart, and sociable companion dog with the hypoallergenic coat of the Poodle. The calm and gentle nature of the Newfoundland and the Poodle's intellect and low-shedding qualities combined to make the Newfypoo an appealing option for dog enthusiasts looking for a family-friendly and hypoallergenic canine.

Newfypoo / KimStone214 / Shutterstock.com

What is Unique about the Newfypoo

The Newfypoo boasts an array of distinct characteristics that set it apart from other dogs. First and foremost, their size is imposing; with weights that can span anywhere between 70 to 150 pounds (31 to 68 kilograms) or even more. This formidable size, coupled with their robust build, gives the Newfypoo a majestic presence. Their coats, which can vary from curly, wavy, to straight, often reflect the hypoallergenic properties from their Poodle lineage. This coat comes in an array of hues, from blacks and browns to pristine whites, sometimes combined in beautiful patterns.

At their core, Newfypoos have temperaments that are nothing short of endearing. They often exude the gentle, calm, and patient demeanor associated with the Newfoundland, endearing them to families and making them exceptional candidates for therapy roles. Their intelligence, another inheritance from their Poodle ancestors, is evident in their quick learning abilities. They respond enthusiastically to positive reinforcement, highlighting their trainability. But perhaps one of their most cherished traits is their affinity for water. Many Newfypoos, courtesy of their Newfoundland roots, are natural water enthusiasts. Whether it's swimming, fetching in water bodies, or simply splashing around, these dogs revel in water-based activities, making them the perfect companions for beach outings or lakeside retreats.

Temperament and Personality of the Newfypoo

Newfypoos, often referred to as "gentle giants," truly live up to their title. These magnificent dogs are celebrated for their gentle and patient disposition, a trait that endears them to families, especially those with young children and other pets. Their amiable nature extends beyond their immediate family, as they frequently exhibit warmth and friendliness even towards strangers. Their sociable character and affectionate tendencies mean they thrive on human interaction and are happiest when surrounded by their loved ones.

However, it isn't just their amiability that stands out. Newfypoos are incredibly sharp, a characteristic they inherit from their Poodle ancestors. This intelligence, paired with their eagerness to please, makes them a joy to train. Positive reinforcement methods resonate well with them, and they delight in activities that stimulate their minds. Despite their friendly demeanor, Newfypoos possess a protective streak. They are instinctively watchful over their family, and while they aren't known for being aggressive, their imposing size coupled with a deep, resonant bark can be a formidable deterrent to any potential threats.

Furthermore, the Newfypoo's calming and patient demeanor lends itself beautifully to therapeutic roles. Many individuals find solace in the comforting presence of a Newfypoo. Their innate ability to provide emotional support and their unassuming nature make them exceptional therapy dogs, offering solace and companionship to those in need.

Care for the Newfypoo

Proper care is essential to ensure the health and well-being of your Newfypoo. Here are some aspects to consider when caring for your Newfypoo:

1. Feeding: Provide your Newfypoo with a balanced and nutritious diet suitable for its size, age, and activity level. Consult with your veterinarian to determine the appropriate amount and type of food to feed your dog. Avoid overfeeding to prevent weight gain and associated health problems.

2. Exercise: While Newfypoos are generally calm and relaxed indoors, they still require regular exercise to maintain their physical and mental health. Daily walks, playtime, and activities such as swimming can help meet their exercise needs. However, avoid overexertion, especially in hot weather, due to their thick coat.
3. Grooming: The grooming needs of a Newfypoo can vary depending on the type of coat it inherits. Regular brushing is typically necessary to prevent matting and tangling of the fur. Professional grooming may be required every few months to maintain a neat appearance and ensure proper coat care.
4. Health Problems: Like all dog breeds, Newfypoos can be prone to certain health issues. Common concerns may include hip dysplasia, elbow dysplasia, heart conditions, eye problems, and certain genetic disorders inherited from their parent breeds. Regular vet check-ups, a nutritious diet, exercise, and maintaining a healthy weight can help minimize the risk of these problems.

Training the Newfypoo

Training a Newfypoo requires an early start, preferably during their puppyhood, to instill foundational obedience and social skills. These dogs thrive on positive reinforcement methods, with treats, praise, and rewards effectively motivating them to learn. However, it's important for owners to remain consistent and patient throughout the training process. Given that some Newfypoos can be slower to mentally mature, maintaining calmness and persistence is vital. Properly socializing them by exposing them to diverse people, animals, and situations ensures they grow into confident and well-adjusted dogs, minimizing potential behavioral issues down the line.

Benefits of the Newfypoo

The Newfypoo offers several benefits to potential owners:

1. Hypoallergenic Coat: Many Newfypoos inherit the low-shedding and hypoallergenic coat from their Poodle parent, making them suitable for individuals with allergies or sensitivities to dog hair.
2. Family-Friendly: Newfypoos are generally known for their gentle and friendly nature, making them great companions for families with children and other pets.
3. Intelligence and Trainability: With their Poodle lineage, Newfypoos are intelligent and trainable dogs. They excel in various training activities and tasks, including obedience, agility, and even therapy work.
4. Versatility: Newfypoos come in different sizes, depending on the size of the Poodle parent used in breeding. This allows potential owners to choose a size that fits their lifestyle and living arrangements, whether that be a standard, miniature, or even a toy-sized Newfypoo.

Interesting Facts about the Newfypoo

1. The Newfypoo's name is a combination of "Newfoundland," referring to one parent breed, and "Poodle."
2. Newfypoos can come in a wide range of coat colors, including black, brown, white, and various combinations, adding to their visual appeal.
3. Due to their large size and strength, Newfypoos can excel in activities such as water rescue, cart-pulling, and other working roles.
4. Newfypoos are known for their calm and patient temperament,

making them well-suited as therapy dogs, providing comfort and companionship to those in need.
5. Some Newfypoos inherit the Poodle's intelligence and the Newfoundland's natural instincts for water rescue, making them excellent candidates for water sports and activities.
6. The popularity of Newfypoos has led to the establishment of breed-specific rescue organizations that specialize in finding homes for Newfypoos in need.

These facts and traits contribute to the appeal of the Newfypoo as a lovable, intelligent, and versatile companion for many dog lovers.

Pinny-poo

History of the Pinny-poo

The Pinny-poo is an intriguing hybrid breed that combines the traits of a Miniature Pinscher and a Poodle. This breed originated more recently as part of the designer dog trend, which emerged in the late 20th century. The specific origins and timeline of the Pinny-poo are not well-documented, but it is believed to have gained popularity in the United States and other countries over the past couple of decades.

The aim of breeding the Pinny-poo was to create a dog that combined the desirable characteristics of both parent breeds. The Miniature Pinscher is known for its lively and spirited nature, while the Poodle brings intelligence and a hypoallergenic coat to the mix. By crossing these two breeds, breeders sought to produce a small, energetic companion dog with a low-shedding coat.

Pinny-poo / DogBreedInfo.com

What is Unique about the Pinny-poo

The Pinny-poo boasts a range of appealing characteristics that make them a unique and cherished breed. With their small to medium stature, standing at 10 to 15 inches and weighing 10 to 20 pounds, they're an ideal companion for those living in apartments or homes with limited space. Their coat, often taking after the Poodle's curly or wavy texture, not only presents hypoallergenic properties, minimizing shedding and allergies, but also comes in a variety of colors, enhancing their visual charm.

Yet, it's not just their size and coat that make them stand out. Infused with the energy and agility of the Miniature Pinscher, Pinny-poos are spirited and playful, requiring regular exercise and active play sessions. This zest for life makes them a fantastic companion for energetic owners or those who revel in involving their dogs in dynamic activities. Furthermore, their Poodle lineage ensures they possess a keen intellect. Quick to learn and ever-curious, these dogs thrive when mentally engaged, be it through training, canine sports, or interactive toys and games.

Temperament and Personality of the Pinny-poo

Many people adore the distinctive temperament and characteristics of the Pinny-poo mix. The Pinny-poo exudes an undeniable passion for life since it shares the Miniature Pinscher's vibrant and animated personality. There is never a dull moment for their owners thanks to these curious dogs who are constantly alert and eager to investigate every corner of their environment.

The Pinny-poo's sharp mind is comparable to that of the famed Poodle. These dogs are intelligent and observant in addition to being lively, and their owners are frequently taken aback by how quickly they pick things up. Positive reinforcement approaches make it easier to train a Pinny-poo by enhancing their receptivity and desire to please. They make a loving and faithful companion thanks to their loyalty and intellect. Pinny-poos exhibit an endearing kind of steadfast affection that shows how much they value the relationship they develop with their owners.

But these dogs aren't just for love and play; they also have a defensive streak because to their Miniature Pinscher ancestry. Even while they normally get along with family members, including kids and other pets, they can be suspicious of strangers. They may not be big, but they can still act as a watchdog to make sure their loved ones are always protected because to their attentiveness and propensity to bark at any threats.

Care for the Pinny-poo

1. Feeding: Providing a well-balanced diet is crucial for the overall health and well-being of the Pinny-poo. High-quality dog food appropriate for their size, age, and activity level should be selected. It is important to follow feeding guidelines and monitor their weight to prevent obesity.
2. Exercise: Pinny-poos have moderate exercise needs. Daily walks, play sessions, and interactive toys will help meet their energy requirements. Mental stimulation through training exercises or puzzle toys is also beneficial.
3. Grooming: The Pinny-poo's coat requires regular maintenance. If they have inherited the Poodle's curly or wavy coat, brushing every few days is necessary to prevent matting and tangles. Regular professional grooming appointments may also be required to maintain a well-groomed appearance.
4. Health Problems: As with any breed, Pinny-poos can be prone to certain health issues. While hybrid vigor may reduce the risk of inheriting specific conditions, it is important to be aware of potential health concerns in both parent breeds. Regular vet check-ups, a balanced diet, exercise, and preventive care can help ensure their overall well-being.

Training the Pinny-poo

Training a Pinny-poo should begin early and focus on positive reinforcement techniques. They are intelligent and eager to please, making them quick learners. Consistency, patience, and using rewards such as treats and praise will encourage their cooperation and help establish a strong bond with their owner.

Socialization is equally important to help the Pinny-poo become well-rounded and confident. Exposing them to various people, animals, and environments from a young age will help them develop good manners and adaptability.

Benefits of the Pinny-poo

The Pinny-poo offers several benefits to potential owners:

1. Hypoallergenic Coat: Many Pinny-poos have a low-shedding, hypoallergenic coat inherited from the Poodle parent. This makes them a suitable choice for individuals with allergies or sensitivities to dog hair.
2. Size: The Pinny-poo's small to medium size makes them adaptable to different living situations, including apartments or homes with limited space.
3. Intelligence and Trainability: With their Poodle heritage, Pinny-poos are intelligent and trainable. They excel in obedience training, agility, and other canine activities that challenge their minds.
4. Companionable Nature: Pinny-poos are affectionate and devoted companions. They form strong bonds with their owners and enjoy being part of the family.

Interesting Facts about the Pinny-poo

1. The Pinny-poo's name combines "Pinny," referring to the Miniature Pinscher, and "Poo" from Poodle, reflecting their parentage.
2. Pinny-poos can have a variety of coat colors and patterns, depending on the genes inherited from their parents. These can include black, brown, cream, or a combination of these colors.
3. Pinny-poos often exhibit a playful and mischievous nature, inherited from the Miniature Pinscher parent.
4. They can be excellent watchdogs, alerting their owners to potential intruders with their sharp barks.
5. Pinny-poos are generally long-lived dogs, with an average lifespan of 12 to 15 years.
6. As a mixed breed, Pinny-poos can exhibit a wide range of physical and temperamental traits, even within the same litter.
7. Pinny-poos may vary in size depending on the size of the Poodle parent. Breeding with Toy or Miniature Poodles can result in smaller Pinny-poos, while breeding with Standard Poodles can produce larger ones.

Remember, as the Pinny-poo is a relatively new hybrid breed, individual dogs may vary in appearance and temperament. It is essential to research and interact with reputable breeders or rescue organizations to ensure you find a healthy and well-socialized Pinny-poo that suits your lifestyle.

Pomapoo

History of the Pomapoo

The Pomapoo is a hybrid breed that combines the Pomeranian and the Poodle. It is part of the designer dog trend that emerged in recent years, aiming to create unique and desirable crossbreeds. While the exact origins of the Pomapoo are unclear, it is believed to have originated in the United States, like many other poodle hybrids, during the late 20th or early 21st century.

The Pomeranian, originating from the region of Pomerania in Europe, is known for its small size, fox-like appearance, and spirited personality. On the other hand, the Poodle, originally from Germany, is highly regarded for its intelligence, hypoallergenic coat, and versatility. By combining these two breeds, breeders sought to create a dog that would possess the Pomeranian's adorable looks and playful nature, along with the Poodle's intelligence and low-shedding coat.

What is Unique about the Pomapoo

The Pomapoo stands out due to its adorable and distinctive appearance. As a crossbreed, the Pomapoo can exhibit a variety of physical traits, including variations in size, coat type, and color. They often inherit the Pomeranian's compact size and the Poodle's curly or wavy, low-shedding coat. This combination results in a charming and fluffy companion that attracts many dog lovers.

Another unique aspect of the Pomapoo is its lively and affectionate personality. These dogs are known for their playful nature and love to be the center of attention. They often form strong bonds with their owners and enjoy being part of a family. Pomapoos have a zest for life and can bring a lot of joy and entertainment to their households.

Temperament and Personality of the Pomapoo

Pomapoos are typically friendly, sociable, and intelligent dogs. They often inherit the Poodle's intelligence and the Pomeranian's lively and alert nature. These traits make them quick learners and eager to please their owners. Pomapoos tend to be affectionate and enjoy spending time with their families. They are known to be good with children and can get along well with other pets if properly socialized from a young age.

Despite their small size, Pomapoos can have a confident and spirited personality. They are often curious and enjoy exploring their surroundings. While they may have a touch of Pomeranian's tendency to be vocal, Pomapoos can be trained to control excessive barking through consistent and positive reinforcement training methods.

Care for the Pomapoo

1. Feeding: Pomapoos require a balanced diet to maintain their health. It is important to provide them with high-quality dog food that suits their age, size, and activity level. Consult with a veterinarian to determine the appropriate portion sizes and feeding schedule for your Pomapoo.

2. Exercise: Despite their small size, Pomapoos have moderate exercise needs. Daily walks, interactive playtime, and mental stimulation activities, such as puzzle toys or obedience training sessions, are essential to keep them physically and mentally engaged. However, it's important not to overexert them due to their small stature.
3. Grooming: Pomapoos often have a wavy or curly coat that requires regular grooming. Brushing their coat a few times a week helps prevent matting and keeps their fur looking its best. Professional grooming, including hair trimming and nail clipping, may be required every few months. Additionally, regular dental care, ear cleaning, and occasional bathing are important for their overall hygiene.
4. Health Problems: Pomapoos, like any other dog breed, can be prone to certain health issues. Some common health concerns include dental problems, patellar luxation (knee dislocation), eye issues, and allergies. Regular veterinary check-ups, maintaining good dental hygiene, and providing a healthy diet and lifestyle can help minimize the risk of these problems.

Training the Pomapoo

Training a Pomapoo should start early and focus on positive reinforcement techniques. They are intelligent dogs and respond well to rewards such as treats, praise, and playtime. Early socialization is crucial to help them develop good manners and become well-rounded dogs. Consistency, patience, and a gentle approach will yield the best results in training a Pomapoo.

Benefits of the Pomapoo

The Pomapoo offers several benefits to potential owners:

1. Adaptability: Due to their small size, Pomapoos can adapt well to various living situations, including apartments and houses.
2. Intelligence: Pomapoos inherit the intelligence of both parent breeds, making them trainable and able to learn new commands and tricks quickly.
3. Companionship: Pomapoos are often devoted to their families and can provide loyal companionship. They thrive on human interaction and enjoy being involved in their owners' daily activities.
4. Low-shedding: The Poodle influence on the Pomapoo's coat often results in a low-shedding or hypoallergenic coat, making them suitable for individuals with allergies or those who prefer a cleaner living environment.

Interesting Facts about the Pomapoo

1. Pomapoos are sometimes referred to as "Poos" or "Poodle Pomeranians."
2. Their small size and adorable appearance make them popular choices for celebrities and individuals seeking a fashionable and portable companion.
3. Pomapoos can come in a variety of colors, including black, white, cream, brown, or a combination of these.
4. Some Pomapoos may have a tendency to exhibit the "small dog syndrome" if not properly trained and socialized, which can lead to behavioral issues. Early training and socialization are crucial to prevent this.

5. Due to their Pomeranian lineage, Pomapoos may be prone to excessive barking. Consistent training and providing mental stimulation can help manage this behavior.
6. Pomapoos often excel in various canine sports and activities, such as agility and obedience competitions, thanks to their intelligence and agility.
7. Despite their small size, Pomapoos can make excellent watchdogs, as they are alert and tend to be vocal when sensing potential threats.

The Pomapoo is a delightful and charming companion that combines the best traits of the Pomeranian and the Poodle. Their small size, intelligence, and affectionate nature make them a popular choice for many dog lovers seeking a loyal and lovable pet.

Pomapoochon

History of the Pomapoochon

The Pomapoochon, also known as the Pomeranian Poodle Bichon mix, is a delightful hybrid breed that combines the Pomeranian, Poodle, and Bichon Frise. While the exact origin of the Pomapoochon is not well-documented, it is believed to have emerged in recent years as part of the designer dog trend, which aims to create unique and desirable traits by crossing different purebred dogs.

The Pomapoochon's lineage can be traced back to the Pomeranian, a small toy breed known for its lively personality and fluffy coat. Poodles, with their intelligence and hypoallergenic traits, were then introduced into the mix. The Bichon Frise, a cheerful and affectionate breed, was later incorporated to add its charming characteristics. The result is a hybrid breed that captures the best traits of its parent breeds.

What is Unique about the Pomapoochon

The Pomapoochon is capturing the hearts of many with its unique attributes and undeniable charm. Nestled within a small frame, typically weighing just between 5 to 15 pounds, this breed is perfect for those living in confined spaces such as apartments. Their compact size, however, does not compromise on their striking appearance. With a coat that can vary from curly to wavy or even straight, it boasts a soft and fluffy texture, akin to a plush toy. Regular grooming is paramount to ensure it remains pristine and lustrous.

What further distinguishes the Pomapoochon is the myriad of colors their coat can manifest in. From pristine whites and creamy hues to deep blacks, browns, and the enchanting sable, they offer a palette that caters to a diverse range of individual tastes. But it isn't just about aesthetics with the Pomapoochon; practicality is also interwoven into their allure. The infusion of Poodle and Bichon Frise genetics bestows upon some Pomapoochons hypoallergenic qualities. While it's not universal across all members of the breed, many Pomapoochons tend to shed less and produce fewer allergens, providing a potential reprieve for those dog enthusiasts who suffer from allergies. The Pomapoochon, with its alluring blend of beauty and function, truly stands out as a gem in the canine world.

Temperament and Personality of the Pomapoochon

The Pomapoochon has carved a niche for itself in the hearts of many with its exuberant personality and endearing nature. Known for being playful and energetic, the Pomapoochon is always ready for a game or an adventure, filling homes with laughter and joy. Their zest for life is contagious, always looking for ways to engage in activities that challenge both their mind and body.

But it's not just their playful nature that stands out; their intelligence is remarkable. Thanks to the infusion of Poodle and Bichon Frise genetics, these little furballs are not just quick learners but also highly observant of their environment. This acute alertness, combined with their loyalty, makes them surprisingly effective watchdogs. While they may not be intimidating due to their petite size, their keen sense of awareness ensures they're quick to notify their family of any unusual activities.

At their core, Pomapoochons are deeply social and loving creatures. They have an innate ability to bond deeply with their human counterparts, becoming an inseparable part of their lives. This bond of loyalty and affection extends beyond their human family; they are generally congenial with both children and other pets. Proper socialization from a young age ensures that Pomapoochons fit seamlessly into households, endearing themselves to all and becoming cherished companions for young and old alike.

Care for the Pomapoochon

To ensure the Pomapoochon's overall well-being, proper care is essential. Here are some key aspects of caring for a Pomapoochon:

1. Feeding: Provide your Pomapoochon with a balanced diet that meets their nutritional needs. The specific feeding requirements may vary based on their age, size, and activity level. Consult with a veterinarian to determine the appropriate diet plan for your dog.
2. Exercise: Despite their small size, Pomapoochons require regular exercise to maintain a healthy weight and mental stimulation. Daily walks, play sessions, and interactive toys can help fulfill their exercise needs. Be mindful not to overexert them due to their size and potential respiratory concerns associated with brachycephalic traits.
3. Grooming: The Pomapoochon's coat may require regular grooming to keep it clean, tangle-free, and in good condition. Brushing their coat a few times a week helps prevent matting and keeps their fur looking its best. Regular nail trims, ear cleaning, and

dental care are also essential for their overall hygiene.
4. Health Problems: Pomapoochons may be susceptible to certain health issues commonly found in their parent breeds, such as dental problems, luxating patellas, hip dysplasia, eye disorders, and allergies. Regular veterinary check-ups, maintaining good oral hygiene, and addressing any health concerns promptly can help mitigate potential problems.

Training the Pomapoochon

Training a Pomapoochon requires an early start, emphasizing positive reinforcement techniques like treats and praise to harness their eagerness to please. Essential commands, including sit, stay, and leash walking, should be introduced patiently and consistently, with training sessions kept short to maintain their attention. Equally crucial is early socialization, exposing the Pomapoochon to various people, environments, and animals, ensuring they develop confidence and adaptability. Given their innate intelligence, it's beneficial to engage them in ongoing mental stimulation, be it through puzzle toys, obedience classes, or agility training, to keep them mentally engaged and ward off boredom.

Benefits of the Pomapoochon

Owning a Pomapoochon comes with several benefits that make them an appealing choice for many dog lovers:

1. Companionship: Pomapoochons are loving and devoted companions that form strong bonds with their owners. They thrive on human interaction and provide constant companionship and emotional support.

2. Adaptability: Due to their small size, Pomapoochons can adapt well to various living arrangements, including apartments or homes with limited space. They can be suitable for both individuals and families.
3. Low-Shedding Coat: While not all Pomapoochons are guaranteed to be hypoallergenic, their coat tends to shed less than some other breeds. This can be advantageous for individuals who have allergies or prefer a cleaner living environment.
4. Playful and Energetic: Pomapoochons have an enthusiastic and playful nature, making them great playmates and sources of entertainment. Their energy can brighten up any household and bring joy to their owners' lives.

Interesting Facts about the Pomapoochon

1. Pomapoochons are often referred to as "designer dogs" due to their hybrid nature, which combines three distinct purebred breeds.
2. Their appearance can vary widely, even within the same litter, as they may inherit different traits from their parent breeds.
3. Pomapoochons are known to be adaptable to different climates, making them suitable for various regions and weather conditions.
4. Due to their intelligence and eagerness to please, Pomapoochons can excel in obedience training, agility trials, and other canine sports.
5. Pomapoochons tend to be expressive and may communicate their emotions through various vocalizations, including barks, howls, and whines.
6. They are generally sociable dogs and enjoy spending time with their families, participating in activities, and being the center of attention.
7. Pomapoochons have a relatively long lifespan, ranging from 12 to

16 years, with proper care and a healthy lifestyle.

Remember, the specific traits and characteristics of a Pomapoochon can vary depending on the individual dog and the mix of its parent breeds. It is essential to spend time with and get to know your Pomapoochon to understand its unique personality and care requirements.

Pomskydoodle

History of the Pomskydoodle

The Pomskydoodle is a captivating hybrid breed that has gained popularity in recent years. It is a cross between a Pomeranian and a Siberian Husky, with the addition of Poodle genes to create the Pomskydoodle. While the exact origins of the Pomskydoodle are not well-documented, it is believed to have emerged during the early 2000s in the United States, as part of the designer dog trend.

The breeding of Pomskydoodles aimed to combine the appealing traits of both parent breeds. Pomeranians are known for their small size, lively personalities, and luxurious coats, while Siberian Huskies are known for their striking appearance, endurance, and friendly nature. By incorporating Poodle genetics into the mix, breeders hoped to create a smaller-sized dog with a striking appearance, a friendly temperament, and potentially hypoallergenic qualities.

What is Unique about the Pomskydoodle

The Pomskydoodle stands out due to its unique combination of features inherited from its parent breeds. Their small to medium size, typically ranging from 10 to 30 pounds, makes them a perfect companion for those with limited living space, such as condo or apartment dwellers. This breed showcases a plethora of coat colors and patterns, taking after the thick, plush double coat of the Husky and often exhibiting colors like black, white, or gray. Their fox-like features, including erect ears and captivating eyes, add to their undeniable charm. Beyond their looks, Pomskydoodles have a temperament that combines the best of their lineage. Their lively, affectionate disposition stems from the friendly Pomeranian traits and the sociable nature of the Siberian Husky, resulting in a playful dog that cherishes family time. Furthermore, the introduction of Poodle genes into the mix offers potential hypoallergenic benefits, which is a welcome trait for allergy sufferers, as this may mean reduced shedding and less dander.

Temperament and Personality of the Pomskydoodle

Pomskydoodles, with their lively personality, are a welcome addition to many homes. Their fun and energetic personalities ensure that they are always up for a game, and they lend a young flair to any home. This vitality, combined with their great intelligence and curiosity, indicates that they are not just physically active but also mentally agile. They are fast to investigate their surroundings and eager to learn, making them highly responsive to teaching, particularly when positive reinforcement methods are applied. Pomskydoodles have a gregarious and affectionate side aside from their lively antics and bright wits. They value the relationships they make with their families and thrive on the attention and company they receive. Their kind demeanor, when combined with adequate socialization, enables them to get along well with youngsters and other household pets.

Care for the Pomskydoodle

To ensure the health and well-being of your Pomskydoodle, it is important to provide them with proper care and attention. Here are some essential aspects of caring for a Pomskydoodle:

1. Feeding: Pomskydoodles require a well-balanced diet that is appropriate for their age, size, and activity level. Consult with your veterinarian to determine the best feeding routine and choose high-quality dog food that meets their nutritional needs.
2. Exercise: Pomskydoodles are energetic dogs that benefit from regular exercise and mental stimulation. Daily walks, play sessions, and interactive toys can help meet their exercise requirements and prevent boredom. Engaging them in activities that challenge their intelligence and problem-solving skills is also beneficial.
3. Grooming: The grooming needs of Pomskydoodles may vary depending on the type of coat they inherit. Regular brushing is generally required to prevent matting and to keep their fur clean and healthy. Additionally, periodic professional grooming may be necessary to maintain their coat's appearance. Nails should be trimmed regularly, teeth should be brushed, and ears should be checked for cleanliness to prevent any potential issues.
4. Health Problems: Pomskydoodles, like any breed, may be prone to certain health issues. Potential health concerns can include hip dysplasia, patellar luxation, dental problems, and eye conditions. Regular veterinary check-ups, maintaining a healthy weight, and providing appropriate preventive care can help minimize the risk of these problems.

Training the Pomskydoodle

Training a Pomskydoodle requires an early start, emphasizing the importance of early socialization to ensure they grow confident and well-adjusted. Employing positive reinforcement techniques, like rewards and praise, capitalizes on their intelligence and responsiveness. Consistency in commands and cues, coupled with patience, is paramount for effective training, while avoiding punishment-based approaches. Moreover, broadening their exposure to various people, animals, and environments will further enhance their sociability and reduce potential behavioral issues.

Benefits of the Pomskydoodle

The Pomskydoodle offers several benefits to potential owners:

1. Adorable Appearance: With their charming looks, fluffy coats, and striking eyes, Pomskydoodles are undeniably adorable and can bring joy to any household.
2. Lively and Playful Nature: Pomskydoodles have an energetic and playful temperament, making them delightful companions for active individuals or families with children.
3. Potential Hypoallergenic Qualities: Due to the Poodle genetics in their lineage, some Pomskydoodles may have low-shedding or hypoallergenic qualities. This can be beneficial for individuals with allergies or sensitivities to dog hair.
4. Family-Friendly: Pomskydoodles are often known for their sociability and compatibility with children and other pets when properly socialized. They can make loving and loyal family pets.
5. Intelligence and Trainability: Pomskydoodles inherit intelligence from both the Pomeranian and the Poodle, making them trainable

and adaptable to various training activities and tasks.

Interesting Facts about the Pomskydoodle

1. Pomskydoodle is a portmanteau of "Pomeranian," "Siberian Husky," and "Poodle," reflecting the breeds involved in their lineage.
2. The size of Pomskydoodles can vary widely, as it depends on the size of the Pomeranian and Husky parents used in the breeding process.
3. Pomskydoodles are often sought after due to their resemblance to miniature versions of Huskies, capturing the attention of Husky enthusiasts who desire a smaller-sized dog.
4. Each Pomskydoodle can have a unique appearance, with variations in coat colors, patterns, and facial features inherited from their parent breeds.
5. Pomskydoodles can exhibit a range of vocalizations, including barking, howling, and "talking" like their Husky ancestors.
6. Pomskydoodles thrive on mental stimulation and require regular exercise to prevent behavioral issues that can arise from boredom or pent-up energy.
7. The popularity of Pomskydoodles has led to an increase in dedicated breeders who aim to produce healthy and well-tempered puppies of this hybrid breed.

These details provide a comprehensive overview of the Pomskydoodle breed, covering its history, unique traits, temperament, care requirements, training, benefits, and interesting facts. By including this information in your book, readers will gain a deeper understanding of the fascinating Pomskydoodle breed and its characteristics.

Saint Berndoodle

History of the Saint Berdoodle

The Saint Berdoodle is a hybrid breed that combines the Saint Bernard and the Poodle. It is a relatively new designer breed that has gained popularity in recent years. The exact origins of the Saint Berdoodle are unclear, but it is believed to have emerged in the United States during the 1980s or 1990s when the trend of creating crossbreeds became popular.

The goal of breeding the Saint Berdoodle was to combine the desirable traits of both parent breeds. The Saint Bernard is known for its gentle and patient nature, as well as its ability to be a great family dog. On the other hand, the Poodle is highly intelligent, hypoallergenic, and has a low-shedding coat. By crossing these two breeds, breeders aimed to create a dog with the Saint Bernard's friendly temperament and the Poodle's hypoallergenic qualities.

Saint Berndoodle

What is Unique about the Saint Berdoodle

The Saint Berdoodle stands out due to its unique appearance and coat. It typically inherits the wavy or curly, low-shedding coat of the Poodle, which makes it an excellent choice for individuals with allergies. The coat can come in various colors, including black, brown, apricot, and white, among others. The combination of these colors adds to the breed's visual appeal.

Another unique aspect of the Saint Berdoodle is its size. As a crossbreed, the size of Saint Berdoodles can vary depending on the size of the Poodle used in the breeding process. They can range from small to large, depending on whether a Miniature, Medium, or Standard Poodle is used as one of the parent breeds.

Temperament and Personality of the Saint Berdoodle

Saint Berdoodles are known for their friendly and gentle nature, much like their Saint Bernard parent. They are often described as loyal, affectionate, and good-natured dogs. With the combination of their Saint Bernard and Poodle heritage, they tend to be loving and devoted to their families, making them excellent companions.

Saint Berdoodles are generally intelligent dogs and quick learners. They are known to be good with children and can get along well with other pets if properly socialized from an early age. Their patient and gentle demeanor make them suitable for families and individuals looking for a loving and loyal companion.

Care for the Saint Berdoodle

1. Feeding: Saint Berdoodles require a well-balanced diet to maintain their health. It is important to provide them with high-quality dog food that meets their nutritional needs. The specific feeding requirements may vary based on the size, age, and activity level of the individual dog. Consult with a veterinarian to determine the appropriate diet for your Saint Berdoodle.
2. Exercise: While Saint Berdoodles are not as active as some other breeds, they still require regular exercise to stay healthy and prevent obesity. Daily walks and playtime are essential to keep them physically and mentally stimulated. However, it is important to be mindful of their size and not overexert them, especially when they are young and still developing.
3. Grooming: The grooming needs of Saint Berdoodles depend on the type of coat they inherit. If they have a curly or wavy coat, regular brushing is necessary to prevent matting and keep their fur tangle-free. Additionally, they may require occasional

professional grooming to maintain a well-groomed appearance. It is also important to keep their ears clean and check their eyes regularly.
4. Health Problems: Like all breeds, Saint Berdoodles can be prone to certain health issues. Some common health concerns include hip dysplasia, elbow dysplasia, bloat, ear infections, and certain genetic disorders inherited from their parent breeds. Regular veterinary check-ups, a balanced diet, proper exercise, and maintaining a healthy weight can help minimize the risk of these problems. It is crucial to choose a reputable breeder who performs health screenings on their parent dogs to ensure the overall health of the puppies.

Training the Saint Berdoodle

Training a Saint Berdoodle should start early and focus on positive reinforcement techniques. They are generally intelligent and eager to please, which makes training them a rewarding experience. Early socialization is important to expose them to various people, animals, and environments to help them become well-rounded and confident dogs.

Consistency, patience, and positive reinforcement techniques such as treats, praise, and playtime will yield the best results. Saint Berdoodles can excel in obedience training, agility, and even therapy work due to their gentle nature and intelligence.

Benefits of the Saint Berdoodle

The Saint Berdoodle offers several benefits to potential owners:

1. Hypoallergenic: Many Saint Berdoodles have a low-shedding coat,

making them suitable for individuals with allergies or sensitivities to dog hair.
2. Family-Friendly: Saint Berdoodles are typically friendly and gentle with children and other pets, making them excellent family companions.
3. Intelligence and Trainability: With their Poodle heritage, Saint Berdoodles are intelligent and trainable, which makes them suitable for various training activities and tasks.
4. Size Variability: Saint Berdoodles come in different sizes, depending on the size of the Poodle parent. This allows potential owners to choose a size that fits their lifestyle and living arrangements.

Interesting Facts about the Saint Berdoodle

1. The Saint Berdoodle's name is a combination of "Saint Bernard" and "Poodle."
2. Saint Berdoodles are often referred to as "gentle giants" due to their large size and gentle temperament.
3. They can inherit a variety of coat types, including wavy, curly, or straight, depending on the genetic traits of their parents.
4. Saint Berdoodles are known for their loyalty and protective nature, which makes them good watchdogs.
5. Due to their large size, Saint Berdoodles may require ample space and a securely fenced yard to accommodate their exercise needs.
6. They have a playful side and enjoy interactive games and toys that stimulate their minds.
7. Saint Berdoodles thrive on human companionship and may experience separation anxiety if left alone for long periods.

Remember, it is important to research and consult with reputable breeders or professionals to ensure the well-being of any dog breed, including the Saint Berdoodle.

Schnoodle aka Schnoodlepoo aka Snickerdoodle

History of the Schnoodle

The Schnoodle is a popular hybrid breed that is a cross between a Schnauzer and a Poodle. The exact origins of the Schnoodle are uncertain, but it is believed to have been developed in the late 20th century, following the trend of designer dog breeds. Breeders aimed to combine the desirable traits of the Schnauzer, known for its intelligence and spirited personality, with the Poodle, known for its hypoallergenic coat and intelligence.

The Schnoodle quickly gained popularity as a family pet and companion due to its appealing characteristics. Like other poodle hybrids, such as the Labradoodle and the Goldendoodle, the Schnoodle was created to produce a dog with a low-shedding, hypoallergenic coat that would be suitable for individuals with allergies. This hybrid also aimed to inherit the Schnauzer's intelligence and lively temperament.

Schnoodle / Amie Barron / Shutterstock.com

What is Unique about the Schnoodle

The Schnoodle, a distinctive breed, boasts a coat that varies from wavy to curly, providing potential owners with a choice of appearances. Notably, their coat is typically hypoallergenic and low-shedding, making them ideal for those with allergies. Depending on the Poodle parent's size, Schnoodles can be small to medium-sized, catering to various living conditions and preferences. The breed's intelligence, a blend of the Poodle's and Schnauzer's smarts, ensures they're highly trainable and quick to pick up on commands, often outshining in obedience training and canine activities.

Temperament and Personality of the Schnoodle

Schnoodles, with their radiant energy and spirited disposition, have endeared themselves to families and active individuals alike. Their playful and lively nature, stemming from their inherent zest for life, makes them the perfect companions for those looking for a bit of joy and activity. Yet, it's not just their enthusiasm that stands out; these dogs are deeply sociable creatures. From an early age, if properly socialized, they show a propensity to mix seamlessly with other dogs and pets. This sociability pairs wonderfully with their heartwarming devotion to their owners, a bond that's unmistakable and deeply touching. Their unwavering affection, however, doesn't prevent them from being sharp and watchful. Inheriting the alertness of their Schnauzer ancestors, Schnoodles possess an astute sense of their surroundings. This makes them not just loving companions, but also vigilant watchdogs, ever protective and ready to alert their families of any potential threats.

Care for the Schnoodle

1. Feeding: Providing a well-balanced diet is crucial for the health and well-being of your Schnoodle. Feed them high-quality dog food appropriate for their size, age, and activity level. Consult with your veterinarian for specific dietary recommendations.
2. Exercise: Schnoodles require regular exercise to keep them mentally and physically stimulated. Daily walks, playtime, and interactive toys are essential to meet their exercise needs. Engaging them in activities that challenge their intelligence, such as puzzle toys or training sessions, can also be beneficial.
3. Grooming: The grooming needs of Schnoodles can vary depending on the type of coat they inherit. Regular brushing helps

prevent matting and keeps their fur tangle-free. Some Schnoodles may require professional grooming every few months to maintain a well-groomed appearance.
4. Health Problems: Like any breed, Schnoodles can be prone to certain health issues. Common health concerns include hip dysplasia, progressive retinal atrophy (PRA), and certain genetic disorders inherited from their parent breeds. Regular vet check-ups, a balanced diet, and maintaining a healthy lifestyle can help minimize the risk of these problems.

Training the Schnoodle

Training a Schnoodle is both fun and rewarding. These dogs thrive on positive reinforcement, so it's best to use treats, praise, and playtime as motivators. It's essential to begin socializing them early, exposing them to various people, animals, and environments to boost their confidence and social aptitude. Their intelligence and eagerness to please make them apt pupils for obedience training, starting with basic commands and gradually moving to more complex tasks. For successful training outcomes, maintain consistency in cues and commands and practice patience. Ensuring that the training sessions remain short, engaging, and enjoyable will optimize the learning experience for the Schnoodle.

Benefits of the Schnoodle

The Schnoodle offers several benefits to potential owners:

1. Hypoallergenic: Many Schnoodles have a low-shedding, hypoallergenic coat, making them suitable for individuals with allergies or sensitivities to pet dander.
2. Family-Friendly: Schnoodles are typically friendly and get along

well with children and other pets. They often make excellent family companions and playmates.
3. Intelligence and Trainability: With their Poodle and Schnauzer heritage, Schnoodles are intelligent and trainable. They enjoy mental stimulation and excel in various training activities and tasks.
4. Size Variations: Schnoodles come in different sizes, allowing potential owners to choose a size that suits their living arrangements and lifestyle.

Interesting Facts about the Schnoodle

1. The term "Schnoodle" is a combination of "Schnauzer" and "Poodle," reflecting the breed's mixed lineage.
2. Schnoodles can exhibit a wide range of colors and patterns, including black, white, apricot, and salt and pepper.
3. Some Schnoodles inherit the Schnauzer's distinctive facial hair, known as "beards," which adds to their unique appearance.
4. Schnoodles often have a zest for life and enjoy being part of their families' activities, whether it's going for a hike or simply lounging at home.
5. Due to their hypoallergenic coats and friendly nature, Schnoodles are often used as therapy dogs, bringing comfort and joy to individuals in hospitals, nursing homes, and other care facilities.
6. Schnoodles can participate in various dog sports and activities, such as agility, obedience trials, and scent work, thanks to their intelligence and athleticism.

Remember to thoroughly research and consult with reputable breeders or rescue organizations to ensure you are well-prepared for the responsibilities and needs of owning a Schnoodle.

Sheepadoodle aka Sheepapoo

History of the Sheepadoodle

The Sheepadoodle is a hybrid breed that has gained popularity in recent years. It is a cross between an Old English Sheepdog and a Poodle, typically a Standard Poodle or a Miniature Poodle. While the exact origins of the Sheepadoodle are unclear, it is believed to have originated in the United States during the late 20th century as part of the designer dog trend.

The goal of breeding Sheepadoodles was to combine the desirable traits of both parent breeds. Old English Sheepdogs are known for their intelligence, loyalty, and distinctive appearance with a shaggy coat. Poodles, on the other hand, are highly intelligent, hypoallergenic, and come in different sizes. The aim was to create a dog that possessed the Old English Sheepdog's friendly temperament and distinctive coat while inheriting the Poodle's intelligence and hypoallergenic qualities.

Sheepadoodle / Shutterstock.com

What is Unique about the Sheepadoodle

The Sheepadoodle stands out due to its unique appearance and coat. It inherits the shaggy, low-shedding coat of the Old English Sheepdog, which can vary in texture from wavy to curly. This makes it an excellent choice for individuals with allergies or those who prefer a low-shedding dog. The coat can come in a variety of colors, including black, white, and combinations of both, resembling the Old English Sheepdog's coat. This wide range of colors adds to the breed's uniqueness and visual appeal.

Additionally, Sheepadoodles often inherit the expressive eyes of the Old English Sheepdog, which are known for their warmth and intelligence. These charming eyes, combined with the breed's teddy bear-like appearance, make Sheepadoodles particularly endearing.

Temperament and Personality of the Sheepadoodle

Sheepadoodles are known for their friendly, loving, and affectionate nature. They are often described as being intelligent, gentle, and loyal dogs. With the combination of their Old English Sheepdog and Poodle heritage, they tend to be devoted to their families and get along well with children and other pets. Sheepadoodles are typically eager to please and are quick learners, making them suitable for various training activities.

They can be protective of their families, making them good watchdogs. However, early socialization is crucial to ensure they develop into well-rounded and confident dogs. Sheepadoodles thrive on human companionship and can suffer from separation anxiety if left alone for extended periods. They are happiest when they are part of a loving and active family.

Care for the Sheepadoodle

1. Feeding: Sheepadoodles require a well-balanced diet to maintain their health. It is important to provide them with high-quality dog food that meets their nutritional needs. The specific feeding requirements may vary based on the size, age, and activity level of the individual dog. Consult with a veterinarian to determine the appropriate feeding plan for your Sheepadoodle.
2. Exercise: Sheepadoodles are energetic dogs and require regular exercise to keep them physically and mentally stimulated. Daily walks, playtime, and interactive toys can help meet their exercise needs. They enjoy activities such as fetching, hiking, and agility training. Providing them with opportunities for socialization and mental enrichment is also beneficial for their overall well-being.
3. Grooming: The grooming needs of Sheepadoodles can vary

depending on the type of coat they inherit. If they have a longer, shaggy coat, regular brushing is necessary to prevent matting and to keep their fur tangle-free. Professional grooming may be required every few months to maintain a well-groomed appearance. Additionally, regular ear cleaning, teeth brushing, and nail trimming should be part of their grooming routine.
4. Health Problems: As with any dog breed, Sheepadoodles can be prone to certain health issues. Some common health concerns include hip dysplasia, progressive retinal atrophy (PRA), hypothyroidism, and certain genetic disorders inherited from their parent breeds. Regular vet check-ups, a balanced diet, and maintaining a healthy lifestyle can help minimize the risk of these problems. It is also advisable to choose a reputable breeder who conducts health screenings on the parent dogs.

Training the Sheepadoodle

Training a Sheepadoodle should start early and focus on positive reinforcement techniques. They are intelligent dogs and generally respond well to reward-based training methods. Early socialization is crucial to ensure they develop into well-behaved and well-adjusted dogs. Positive experiences with different people, animals, and environments will help them become confident and adaptable.

Consistency, patience, and using positive reinforcement techniques such as treats, praise, and play will yield the best results. Sheepadoodles have a strong desire to please their owners, making them eager learners. Training sessions should be engaging and mentally stimulating to prevent boredom.

Benefits of the Sheepadoodle

The Sheepadoodle offers several benefits to potential owners:

1. Hypoallergenic: Many Sheepadoodles have a low-shedding coat, making them suitable for individuals with allergies or sensitivities to dog hair. However, it's important to note that no dog breed is completely hypoallergenic, and individual reactions may vary.
2. Family-Friendly: Sheepadoodles are typically friendly, gentle, and patient with children and other pets, making them excellent family companions. They thrive in households where they receive love, attention, and regular exercise.
3. Intelligence and Trainability: With their Poodle heritage, Sheepadoodles are intelligent and trainable, making them suitable for various training activities and tasks. They excel in obedience training and can learn a wide range of commands and tricks.
4. Versatility: Sheepadoodles come in different sizes, ranging from miniature to standard, allowing potential owners to choose a size that fits their lifestyle and living arrangements. Whether living in an apartment or a larger home, there is a Sheepadoodle size suitable for different living environments.

Interesting Facts about the Sheepadoodle

1. The Sheepadoodle's name is a combination of "Sheepdog," referring to the Old English Sheepdog, and "Poodle."
2. The size of Sheepadoodles can vary depending on the size of the Poodle used in the crossbreeding process. Miniature Poodles result in smaller Sheepadoodles, while Standard Poodles produce larger ones.
3. Sheepadoodles have gained popularity due to their hypoallergenic

coat, which makes them a suitable option for individuals who typically experience allergies around dogs.
4. Sheepadoodles are known for their calm and patient nature, making them good therapy dogs. They can provide comfort and emotional support to those in need.
5. Some Sheepadoodles inherit the Poodle's intelligence and herding instincts from the Old English Sheepdog, which can result in a dog that excels in various canine sports and activities.
6. The first-generation Sheepadoodles (F1) are the direct offspring of an Old English Sheepdog and a Poodle. Further breeding can create multigenerational Sheepadoodles (F2, F3, etc.), which can lead to more predictable traits.

The popularity of Sheepadoodles has led to the establishment of breed-specific rescue organizations that specialize in finding homes for Sheepadoodles in need. These organizations play an important role in providing care and finding loving homes for these wonderful hybrid dogs.

Shihpoo

History of the Shihpoo

The Shihpoo is a delightful poodle hybrid that has gained popularity in recent years. It is a crossbreed between a Shih Tzu and a Poodle, usually a Toy Poodle or a Miniature Poodle. While the exact origin of the Shihpoo is uncertain, it is believed to have originated in the United States during the 1980s as part of the designer dog trend.

The purpose of creating the Shihpoo was to combine the desirable traits of both parent breeds. Shih Tzus are known for their affectionate nature and loyalty, while Poodles are intelligent and have a low-shedding coat. Breeders aimed to produce a dog that possessed the Shih Tzu's friendly personality and the Poodle's hypoallergenic coat, making the Shihpoo an attractive choice for individuals with allergies.

Shihpoo

What is Unique about the Shihpoo

The Shihpoo boasts a tapestry of characteristics that make it an endearing and versatile pet. One of its standout features is its coat. Often soft to the touch, the Shihpoo's coat oscillates between wavy to curly textures and is commonly low-shedding. This characteristic makes it an excellent choice for individuals prone to allergies or those who lean towards minimal shedding in their canine companions. In terms of size, the Shihpoo offers a range to suit diverse lifestyles and living conditions. Whether descended from Toy Poodles or Miniature Poodles, there's a Shihpoo size that's bound to fit snugly into one's life. As for its appearance, the Shihpoo is an enchanting medley of its parents. Within a single litter, there can be variations, yet a common theme prevails – the compact, robust frame accentuated by deeply expressive eyes reminiscent of the Shih Tzu, draped in a coat that brings to mind the elegant Poodle.

Temperament and Personality of the Shihpoo

Shihpoos are well recognized for readily winning hearts thanks to their endearing blend of charm and amiability. They have an evident sense of connection at their core. These adorable dogs like receiving attention from people and fit in with families with ease. As they develop strong, enduring ties with their owners, their dedication to them is obvious. This connection transcends simple human interaction. Shihpoos are naturally sociable and frequently get along with kids and other animals. Early socialization makes sure kids develop into well-rounded individuals who enjoy the benefits of interacting with a range of beings, both human and animal.

Their sharp intelligence, which they received from their Poodle ancestry, perfectly complements their caring attitude. Shihpoos have a great capacity for learning new abilities and tricks and are quick and observant learners. Their bright minds respond extraordinarily well to positive reinforcement-based training techniques, and they thrive when given tasks that stretch both their mental and physical capabilities. Their mischievous temperament gives their already endearing demeanor a spice of vivacity. Shihpoos are lively and vivacious animals who enjoy interactive play sessions and enjoy activities that challenge both their minds and bodies equally. They truly exhibit the perfect blending of their parent breeds in their zestful games and perceptive eyes, making them the perfect friends for those who are lucky enough to share their lives with them.

Care for the Shihpoo

Taking care of a Shihpoo involves several aspects, including feeding, exercise, grooming, and monitoring their health.

1. Feeding: Providing a balanced and nutritious diet is essential for the overall health of a Shihpoo. Feeding them high-quality dog food that suits their age, size, and activity level will help maintain their well-being. Consult with a veterinarian to determine the appropriate feeding routine and portion sizes for your Shihpoo.
2. Exercise: While Shihpoos are not as high-energy as some other breeds, they still require regular exercise to keep them healthy and mentally stimulated. Daily walks, interactive play sessions, and occasional visits to a dog park can help fulfill their exercise needs. However, it's important to be mindful of their size and not overexert them.
3. Grooming: The grooming needs of Shihpoos can vary depending on their coat type. Regular brushing is usually necessary to prevent matting and keep their fur in good condition. Professional grooming may be required every few months to maintain a neat and well-groomed appearance. Additionally, regular teeth brushing, ear cleaning, and nail trimming are important parts of their grooming routine.
4. Health Problems: Like any dog breed, Shihpoos may be prone to certain health issues. Some common concerns include dental problems, patellar luxation, eye problems, and allergies. Regular veterinary check-ups, proper dental care, and a healthy lifestyle can help minimize the risk of these health problems. It is advisable to discuss preventive measures and potential health issues with a veterinarian.

Training the Shihpoo

Training a Shihpoo, known for its intelligence and eagerness, should ideally start during their puppy phase. A cornerstone of their training is early socialization; introducing them to varied environments, people, and other animals fosters a confident and socially adept demeanor. As they navigate this expansive world, mastering basic commands such as sit, stay, and leash behaviors is essential. It's imperative to keep these sessions light-hearted and enjoyable, peppering them with treats, praise, and playful rewards to maintain their enthusiasm. House training, another vital aspect, requires a balanced blend of patience and consistency. Celebrate their successful attempts with positive reinforcement to encourage good habits. Beyond these foundational elements, it's crucial to remember that Shihpoos have an inherent need for mental stimulation. Satiate this with a mix of interactive toys, intriguing puzzles, and stimulating training exercises, ensuring their sharp minds are constantly engaged and challenged.

Benefits of the Shihpoo

The Shihpoo offers several benefits to potential owners:

1. Hypoallergenic: Many Shihpoos have a low-shedding and hypoallergenic coat, making them suitable for individuals with allergies or sensitivities to dog hair.
2. Companionable: Shihpoos are known for their friendly and affectionate nature. They often form strong bonds with their owners and make great companions for individuals or families.
3. Adaptability: Shihpoos can adapt well to various living environments, including apartments or houses. Their small size and moderate exercise needs make them suitable for urban living.

4. Intelligence and Trainability: With their Poodle heritage, Shihpoos are intelligent and trainable. They excel in obedience training and enjoy learning new tricks and commands.

Interesting Facts about the Shihpoo

1. The name "Shihpoo" is a combination of "Shih Tzu" and "Poodle," representing the parent breeds.
2. Shihpoos often exhibit a wide range of coat colors, including white, black, cream, brown, and various combinations, adding to their visual appeal.
3. Due to their small size and low-shedding coat, Shihpoos are well-suited for individuals or families living in apartments or those with allergies.
4. Shihpoos are known for their playful and lively personalities, often entertaining their owners with their antics and affectionate nature.
5. As a designer breed, Shihpoos can vary in appearance and temperament, even within the same litter, depending on the traits inherited from their parents.
6. Shihpoos are generally considered to be a healthy breed, but like all dogs, they can be prone to certain genetic health issues. Regular veterinary care and a balanced lifestyle contribute to their overall well-being.
7. Shihpoos may inherit a mix of the Shih Tzu's gentle and affectionate nature and the Poodle's intelligence and hypoallergenic coat, making them a well-rounded and attractive companion.
8. The popularity of Shihpoos has led to increased interest in poodle hybrid breeds, highlighting their appeal as companion animals.

Remember that each individual Shihpoo can have its own unique characteristics and needs, so it's important to get to know your dog as an individual and provide the care and attention that suits them best.

Westiepoo

History of the Westiepoo

The West Highland White Terrier, commonly known as the Westie, is a breed that traces its roots back to Scotland. Originally, these little white dogs were bred for hunting small game in the challenging terrains of the Scottish highlands, their white coats acting as a beacon amidst the rugged landscapes. Their cheerful nature and appealing looks eventually endeared them to many, transforming their role from hunters to beloved companions.

On the other hand, Poodles, renowned for their intelligence and adaptability, come in various sizes from the majestic Standard to the petite Toy. Apart from their brainpower, Poodles are also celebrated for their hypoallergenic coats, which are a blessing for those prone to allergies. They are often seen stealing the limelight in obedience trials, agility courses, and even therapy sessions due to their versatility.

Westiepoo / Camila Mendes / Pexels.com

Merging the endearing qualities of the Westie with the Poodle's hypoallergenic benefits and intelligence gave rise to the Westiepoo. This designer breed, which has gained popularity over the past few decades, encapsulates the best of both worlds, offering a hypoallergenic companion with a captivating personality. While the exact timeline of the Westiepoo's emergence remains a bit ambiguous, it's undeniably a product of the designer dog trend that sought to combine the best traits of its parent breeds.

What is Unique about the Westiepoo

The Westiepoo is a crossbreed with a plethora of charming features. At first glance, their tiny and strong form, evocative of the Westie heritage, is unmistakable. Their coat, dense with waves or curls, comes in a variety of hues ranging from pure white, cream, to a deep black, or a mix, reflecting the rich genetic tapestry they inherit from both parents. Depending on the specific genetic contributions from its Westie and Poodle forebears, each Westiepoo's appearance can be a joyful surprise.

However, aside from its charming look, the Westiepoo has additional characteristics that make them popular with many people. Their hypoallergenic coat, a Poodle ancestor, assures low shedding, making them ideal for allergy patients and those who prefer a cleaner home environment. This, paired with their extraordinary intellect and enthusiasm to learn, makes the Westiepoo an ideal companion for individuals looking for a pet who is both cognitively agile and groomable. They acquire instruction quickly, benefiting from the mental stimulation it provides, and are always eager to learn a new trick or two.

But it is the Westiepoo's friendly and gregarious attitude that actually distinguishes it. They are more than just pets; they become integral family members, blending into the household's regular activities. Their friendly demeanor guarantees that they get along well with children and other pets. However, as with all breeds, early socialization is critical in maintaining the Westiepoo's innate pleasant demeanor and ensuring that the Westiepoo grows into a well-adjusted, lovable companion for all.

Temperament and Personality of the Westiepoo

The Westiepoo is a testament to the beautiful blending of the best qualities of the Westie and Poodle, nestled in the fascinating realm of designer breeds. They have an unending capacity for friendship and an adventurous attitude at their core. A Westiepoo's passionate greeting of a family member or a complete stranger is a charming sight to watch. However, their happy disposition is delicately tempered with a sharp intelligence derived from both of their parent breeds. Whether it's a new command or a cunning prank, these quick learners are always ready for a challenge. Their eager minds respond remarkably well to constructive criticism, with praise and rewards acting as the ideal motivators.

Their intelligence is one of their defining characteristics, but so is their zest for life. The Westiepoo is a vibrant friend and is brimming with energy. Because of their vivacious personality, they require regular exercise to keep their bodies and minds engaged. They are constantly on the go and radiate a youthful excitement, whether it is taking a fast walk around the neighborhood, playing tug of war, or figuring out a puzzle toy. But this lighthearted façade conceals a heart that is intensely devoted. They frequently form an unbreakable link with their human family because of their unconditional love. The Westiepoo enjoys spending time with family and friends and thrives on the attention.

However, they possess a natural awareness inherited from their Westie ancestors that, when necessary, turns these affectionate animals into watchful monitors. They frequently sound the alarm with a strong bark, warning their family of prospective intruders or strange activities in their surroundings. Their sensitive hearing and keen sight rarely miss anything untoward. A magnificent fusion of friendliness, intelligence, loyalty, and protectiveness can be found in Westiepoos, making them a really special companion for those who are fortunate enough to have them in their lives.

Care for the Westiepoo

Caring for a Westiepoo involves several aspects, including feeding, exercise, grooming, and monitoring their health. Here are some guidelines to keep your Westiepoo happy and healthy:

1. Feeding: Provide your Westiepoo with a well-balanced diet that is appropriate for their age, size, and activity level. High-quality dog food, either commercial or homemade, should meet their nutritional needs. Consult your veterinarian for specific feeding recommendations.
2. Exercise: Westiepoos are energetic dogs and require regular exercise to maintain their physical and mental well-being. Daily walks, active playtime, and interactive toys can help fulfill their exercise needs. Mental stimulation, such as puzzle toys and obedience training, is also essential to keep them engaged.
3. Grooming: Westiepoos' grooming needs depend on their coat type and can vary. If they have a wavy or curly coat, regular brushing is necessary to prevent matting and keep their fur tangle-free. Trimming their coat may be required every few months to maintain a well-groomed appearance. Regular grooming sessions should include nail trimming, teeth brushing, and ear cleaning.
4. Health Problems: While Westiepoos are generally healthy dogs, they may be prone to certain health issues inherited from their parent breeds. Common health concerns may include allergies, skin problems, dental issues, and certain genetic conditions. Regular veterinary check-ups, a balanced diet, and maintaining a

healthy lifestyle can help minimize the risk of these problems. It's essential to discuss preventive measures with your veterinarian.

Training the Westiepoo

Training your Westiepoo is instrumental in molding them into a well-behaved and obedient friend, and starting early can lay the foundation for success. Initiating training and socialization from a young age can thwart the development of undesirable habits and establish beneficial behaviors. Given their receptive nature, Westiepoos thrive on positive reinforcement—be it through rewards, treats, or verbal praise, making these tools vital in guiding them during training. Furthermore, clarity and consistency in commands are paramount, as they aid in setting clear expectations and fostering predictable behavior. Simultaneously, a robust socialization process, involving varied interactions with diverse people, animals, and settings, can nurture a confident and balanced temperament in your canine companion. As with any training journey, patience remains key. With persistence and a focus on celebrating the small victories, eschewing punitive methods for more positive, reward-based techniques can pave the way for a harmonious relationship between you and your Westiepoo.

Benefits of the Westiepoo

The Westiepoo offers several benefits to potential owners:

1. Hypoallergenic: Many Westiepoos have a low-shedding coat inherited from the Poodle parent, making them suitable for individuals with allergies or sensitivities to dog hair.
2. Family Companion: Westiepoos are known for their friendly and sociable nature. They often get along well with children and other

pets, making them excellent family companions.
3. Intelligence and Trainability: With the intelligence of both parent breeds, Westiepoos are generally quick learners. They enjoy training sessions and can excel in various training activities and tasks.
4. Size Variations: Westiepoos come in different sizes, depending on the size of the Poodle parent used in the breeding. This allows potential owners to choose a size that suits their living arrangements and lifestyle.

Interesting Facts about the Westiepoo

1. The Westiepoo's name combines "Westie" from West Highland White Terrier and "Poo" from Poodle, reflecting its parent breeds.
2. Westiepoos can vary in size, depending on the Poodle parent. Miniature Poodles result in smaller Westiepoos, while Standard Poodles produce larger ones.
3. Westiepoos have gained popularity due to their hypoallergenic coat, making them suitable for individuals who typically experience allergies around dogs.
4. Some Westiepoos inherit the Poodle's intelligence and the Westie's tenaciousness, making them quick-witted and capable of excelling in activities such as agility and obedience trials.
5. The first-generation Westiepoos (F1) are direct crosses between a Westie and a Poodle. Further breeding can lead to multigenerational Westiepoos (F2, F3, etc.), which may exhibit more consistent traits.
6. Westiepoos often have a charming personality, combining the Westie's playful nature with the Poodle's intelligence and adaptability.

Overall, the Westiepoo is a delightful poodle hybrid breed that brings together the best of both the West Highland White Terrier and the Poodle. With their hypoallergenic coat, friendly temperament, and trainability, Westiepoos make wonderful companions for individuals and families alike.

Whoodle

History of the Whoodle

The Whoodle is a crossbreed between a Soft-Coated Wheaten Terrier and a Poodle. It is part of the growing trend of designer dogs, which aims to combine the desirable characteristics of two different breeds. While the exact origins of the Whoodle are uncertain, it is believed to have emerged in the United States during the late 20th century. The purpose of breeding Whoodles was to create a companion dog that possesses the Poodle's intelligence and hypoallergenic coat, along with the Soft-Coated Wheaten Terrier's friendly and spirited nature.

WHOODLE

Whoodle

What is Unique about the Whoodle

The Whoodle stands out due to its unique combination of traits inherited from its parent breeds. One distinguishing feature is its hypoallergenic coat, which makes it suitable for individuals with allergies or sensitivities to dog hair. The Whoodle's coat can vary, ranging from wavy to curly, and it comes in a variety of colors, including black, brown, cream, and apricot. This wide range of colors adds to the breed's uniqueness and visual appeal.

Temperament and Personality of the Whoodle

Whoodles are known for their friendly, affectionate, and sociable nature. They tend to be outgoing, eager to please, and get along well with people of all ages, including children. The combination of the Soft-Coated Wheaten Terrier's liveliness and the Poodle's intelligence results in a dog that is quick to learn and adaptable. Whoodles often exhibit a playful and energetic demeanor, making them well-suited for families and individuals looking for an active companion.

Care for the Whoodle

1. Feeding: Whoodles require a well-balanced diet to maintain their overall health. It is important to provide them with high-quality dog food that meets their nutritional needs. The specific feeding requirements may vary based on the size, age, and activity level of the individual dog. Consulting with a veterinarian can help determine the appropriate diet for your Whoodle.
2. Exercise: Whoodles are moderately active dogs that require regular exercise to keep them physically and mentally stimulated. Daily walks, playtime, and interactive toys can help meet their

exercise needs. Engaging in activities that provide both physical and mental stimulation, such as puzzle toys or agility training, can be beneficial for their well-being.
3. Grooming: The grooming needs of Whoodles depend on the type of coat they inherit. If they have a wavy or curly coat, regular brushing is necessary to prevent matting and to keep their fur tangle-free. Professional grooming may be required every few months to maintain a well-groomed appearance. Additionally, regular ear cleaning, nail trimming, and teeth brushing should be part of their grooming routine.
4. Health Problems: While hybrid vigor can help reduce the risk of certain genetic health issues, Whoodles may still be prone to certain conditions. Common health concerns include allergies, hip dysplasia, progressive retinal atrophy (PRA), and ear infections. Regular veterinary check-ups, a balanced diet, proper grooming, and maintaining a healthy lifestyle can help minimize the risk of these problems.

Training the Whoodle

Training a Whoodle should start early and focus on positive reinforcement techniques. They are intelligent dogs and generally respond well to reward-based training methods. Consistency, patience, and using positive reinforcement techniques such as treats, praise, and play will yield the best results. Early socialization is essential to help them develop good manners and become well-rounded dogs.

Benefits of the Whoodle

The Whoodle offers several benefits to potential owners:

1. Hypoallergenic: Many Whoodles have a low-shedding coat, making them suitable for individuals with allergies or sensitivities to dog hair.
2. Companionable Nature: Whoodles are known for their friendly and sociable nature. They form strong bonds with their families and enjoy being a part of the household activities.
3. Intelligence and Trainability: With their Poodle heritage, Whoodles are intelligent and trainable. They excel in activities such as obedience training, agility, and even therapy work.
4. Versatility: Whoodles come in different sizes, depending on the size of the Poodle parent used in the crossbreeding process. This allows potential owners to choose a size that fits their lifestyle and living arrangements.

Interesting Facts about the Whoodle

1. The Whoodle's name is a combination of "Wheaten," referring to the Soft-Coated Wheaten Terrier, and "Poodle."
2. Whoodles are often referred to as "designer dogs" due to their intentional crossbreeding and the desire to create a specific combination of traits.
3. The Soft-Coated Wheaten Terrier and Poodle cross results in a dog that tends to have a non-shedding or low-shedding coat, making them a popular choice for individuals with allergies.
4. Whoodles can vary in size, ranging from miniature to standard, depending on the size of the Poodle used in the breeding process.
5. Whoodles are generally social and enjoy spending time with their

families. They may become anxious or develop behavioral issues if left alone for extended periods.
6. Due to their Poodle heritage, Whoodles are often quick learners and can excel in various training activities, including agility, obedience, and even therapy work.
7. Whoodles have a spirited personality and a tendency to exhibit a playful nature, making them well-suited for families with children or individuals seeking an active companion.

The Whoodle's popularity has led to the establishment of breed-specific rescue organizations and reputable breeders who specialize in finding homes for Whoodles in need, promoting responsible ownership and ensuring the well-being of these wonderful hybrid dogs.

Yorkiepoo

History of the Yorkiepoo

The Yorkiepoo is a hybrid breed that has gained popularity in recent years. It is a cross between a Yorkshire Terrier and a Poodle, typically either a Toy Poodle or a Miniature Poodle. While the exact origins of the Yorkiepoo are unclear, it is believed to have originated in the United States during the late 20th century as part of the designer dog trend.

The goal of breeding Yorkiepoos was to combine the desirable traits of both parent breeds. Yorkshire Terriers are known for their lively and affectionate nature, while Poodles are intelligent and hypoallergenic. The aim was to create a dog that possessed the Yorkie's small size and playful personality, along with the Poodle's hypoallergenic coat.

Yorkiepoo

What is Unique about the Yorkiepoo

The Yorkiepoo stands out due to its adorable appearance and coat. It inherits the soft, curly, and low-shedding coat of the Poodle, which makes it a great choice for individuals with allergies or those who prefer a dog with minimal shedding. The coat can come in various colors, including black, white, apricot, and brown, often with markings or patterns resembling the Yorkshire Terrier's coat. This diversity of coat colors adds to the breed's uniqueness and visual appeal.

Temperament and Personality of the Yorkiepoo

Yorkiepoos are known for their friendly and lively nature. They are often described as being affectionate, intelligent, and sociable dogs. With the combination of their Yorkshire Terrier and Poodle heritage, they tend to form strong bonds with their families and enjoy spending time with them. Yorkiepoos are generally good with children and other pets, but early socialization is important to ensure proper behavior. They have a playful and energetic disposition and enjoy interactive play and mental stimulation.

Care for the Yorkiepoo

1. Feeding: Yorkiepoos require a well-balanced diet that is suitable for their size and activity level. It is important to provide them with high-quality dog food that meets their nutritional needs. The specific feeding requirements may vary based on the individual dog, so it is advisable to consult with a veterinarian to determine the appropriate diet.
2. Exercise: While Yorkiepoos are small dogs, they still require regular exercise to keep them healthy and prevent obesity. Daily

walks, playtime, and interactive toys can help meet their exercise needs. However, it's important to avoid overexertion due to their small size and delicate structure.
3. Grooming: The grooming needs of Yorkiepoos depend on the type of coat they inherit. If they have a curly or wavy coat, regular brushing is necessary to prevent matting and to keep their fur tangle-free. Professional grooming may be required every few months to maintain a well-groomed appearance. Regular dental care, nail trimming, and ear cleaning are also essential parts of their grooming routine.
4. Health Problems: Like any breed, Yorkiepoos can be prone to certain health issues. Some common health concerns include dental problems, patellar luxation, eye conditions, and allergies. Regular veterinary check-ups, proper dental care, and a healthy lifestyle can help minimize the risk of these problems. It is also advisable to inquire about the health history of the parent dogs when getting a Yorkiepoo puppy.

Training the Yorkiepoo

Training a Yorkiepoo should start early and focus on positive reinforcement techniques. They are intelligent dogs and generally respond well to reward-based training methods. Yorkiepoos can sometimes have a stubborn streak, so patience, consistency, and positive reinforcement are key. Early socialization is important to expose them to different people, animals, and environments, helping them develop into well-rounded and confident dogs.

Benefits of the Yorkiepoo

The Yorkiepoo offers several benefits to potential owners:

1. Hypoallergenic: Many Yorkiepoos have a low-shedding coat, making them suitable for individuals with allergies or sensitivities to dog hair.
2. Size: Yorkiepoos are small dogs, which makes them well-suited for apartment living or households with limited space. They are also portable and can accompany their owners on various outings.
3. Playful and Lively: Yorkiepoos have a fun-loving and energetic personality, making them enjoyable companions for active individuals or families.
4. Companionability: Yorkiepoos form strong bonds with their families and are known to be loyal and affectionate. They often enjoy being part of their owner's activities and provide companionship.

Interesting Facts about the Yorkiepoo

1. The Yorkiepoo's name is a combination of "Yorkie," referring to the Yorkshire Terrier, and "Poo," derived from the Poodle.
2. Yorkiepoos can come in various sizes depending on the size of the Poodle used in the crossbreeding process. Toy Poodles result in smaller Yorkiepoos, while Miniature Poodles produce larger ones.
3. Yorkiepoos are often sought after due to their hypoallergenic coat, which makes them suitable for individuals who typically experience allergies around dogs.
4. Due to their small size and friendly nature, Yorkiepoos are often used as therapy dogs, providing comfort and companionship to

those in need.
5. Yorkiepoos are generally good with children, but supervision is important due to their small size.
6. Yorkiepoos are known for their intelligence and agility, which makes them capable of participating in various dog sports and activities.
7. The popularity of Yorkiepoos has led to the establishment of breed-specific rescue organizations that specialize in finding homes for Yorkiepoos in need. These organizations provide a valuable resource for individuals interested in adopting a Yorkiepoo.

Yorkiepoochon

History of the Yorkiepoochon

The Yorkiepoochon, also known as the Yorkie Poo Chon or the Teddy Bear, is a delightful hybrid breed that has gained popularity in recent years. It is a crossbreed between a Yorkshire Terrier, a Poodle, and a Bichon Frise. The exact origins of the Yorkiepoochon are not well-documented, but it is believed to have emerged in the early 2000s as part of the designer dog trend, which aimed to create unique and desirable crossbreeds.

The goal of breeding the Yorkiepoochon was to combine the desirable traits of its parent breeds. Yorkshire Terriers are known for their small size, lively personalities, and loyalty. Poodles are highly intelligent, hypoallergenic, and possess an elegant coat. Bichon Frises are cheerful, affectionate, and known for their adorable appearance. By blending these breeds, breeders hoped to create a companion dog that encompassed the best qualities of each breed.

What is Unique about the Yorkiepoochon

The Yorkiepoochon stands out due to its irresistible charm and lovable appearance. One of its distinctive features is its coat, which can be curly, wavy, or straight, depending on the genetic influence of its parents. This breed is highly sought after by individuals with allergies or sensitivities to dog hair, as many Yorkiepoochons have hypoallergenic qualities inherited from the Poodle and Bichon Frise. Their coat colors can vary widely, including combinations of black, brown, white, and various shades of gray.

Another unique aspect of the Yorkiepoochon is its small size. Typically weighing between 6 to 12 pounds and standing around 8 to 12 inches tall, these compact dogs are ideal for apartment living or for those who prefer a smaller companion. Their adorable teddy bear-like appearance, with expressive eyes and a button nose, adds to their overall charm.

Temperament and Personality of the Yorkiepoochon

Yorkiepoochons are known for their affectionate, friendly, and sociable nature. They thrive on human companionship and love being a part of their family's activities. Due to their lineage, they tend to be outgoing, energetic, and playful. They enjoy interactive play sessions and can adapt well to various living situations, whether in a bustling city or a quieter suburban home.

These hybrid dogs are often described as intelligent, alert, and eager to please. They can be quick learners and respond well to positive reinforcement training methods. Yorkiepoochons are generally good with children and other pets, although early socialization is crucial to ensure they develop appropriate behaviors and manners.

Care for the Yorkiepoochon

1. Feeding: Providing a balanced diet is essential for the health and well-being of your Yorkiepoochon. High-quality dog food that meets their nutritional needs, considering their size and activity level, is recommended. Consult with your veterinarian to determine the appropriate feeding schedule and portion sizes.
2. Exercise: Despite their small size, Yorkiepoochons have moderate energy levels and require regular exercise to keep them physically and mentally stimulated. Daily walks, interactive playtime, and engaging toys can help fulfill their exercise needs. Additionally, mental enrichment activities such as puzzle toys and training sessions can help keep their minds sharp.
3. Grooming: The grooming needs of Yorkiepoochons can vary depending on their coat type. If they have a curly or wavy coat, regular brushing is necessary to prevent matting and tangles. Some owners may choose to keep their coat shorter for easier maintenance. It's important to regularly check and clean their ears, trim their nails, and maintain dental hygiene.
4. Health Problems: Like all dog breeds, Yorkiepoochons may be prone to certain health issues. Common concerns can include dental problems, allergies, patellar luxation (kneecap dislocation), and eye conditions. Regular visits to the veterinarian for check-ups and vaccinations, along with a healthy lifestyle, can help prevent and address these potential health problems.

Training the Yorkiepoochon

Training a Yorkiepoochon should start early in their life to establish good behaviors and manners. They are intelligent dogs that respond well to positive reinforcement training methods such as praise, treats, and rewards. Consistency, patience, and a gentle approach are key to their training success. Socialization is also crucial to expose them to different environments, people, and animals, helping them become well-rounded and confident companions.

Benefits of the Yorkiepoochon

The Yorkiepoochon offers several benefits to potential owners:

1. Hypoallergenic: Many Yorkiepoochons inherit hypoallergenic traits from their Poodle and Bichon Frise heritage, making them suitable for individuals with allergies or sensitivities to dog hair.
2. Small Size: The compact size of the Yorkiepoochon makes them a great choice for individuals or families living in apartments or smaller homes.
3. Lively and Affectionate: With their friendly and sociable nature, Yorkiepoochons make excellent companions and thrive on human interaction.
4. Adaptability: Yorkiepoochons can adapt well to different living situations and environments, making them versatile pets for various lifestyles.

Interesting Facts about the Yorkiepoochon

1. The Yorkiepoochon's name reflects the combination of its parent breeds: Yorkshire Terrier, Poodle, and Bichon Frise.
2. Yorkiepoochons are often referred to as "Teddy Bears" due to their resemblance to adorable stuffed toys.
3. Their hypoallergenic coat makes them a popular choice for individuals who typically experience allergies around dogs.
4. Yorkiepoochons are known for their endearing and expressive

facial expressions, which often melt the hearts of their owners.
5. Some Yorkiepoochons have inherited the Poodle's intelligence and agility, making them well-suited for activities such as agility training or canine sports.
6. Yorkiepoochons are generally a healthy breed, but it's important to choose a responsible breeder who conducts health screenings to minimize the risk of hereditary issues.

Overall, the Yorkiepoochon combines the best traits of its parent breeds, resulting in an adorable, affectionate, and versatile companion dog that brings joy and happiness to many families.

Conclusion

"From Poodles to Doodles" took us on an amazing tour into the world of poodle hybrids. We investigated 28 mix breeds, ranging from the intelligent Aussiedoodle to the endearing Yorkipoochon, learning about their rich histories, distinguishing characteristics, temperaments, care requirements, and fascinating facts along the way.

We've looked into the fascinating history of poodle hybrids throughout this book, tracing their origins and learning how they became popular companion animals. We've learned about these breeds' tremendous diversity and versatility, each with its own set of exceptional attributes that set them apart in the canine world.

We've looked at everything from their adorable dispositions and friendly natures to their hypoallergenic coats and low-shedding traits that make poodle hybrids so popular among dog owners. To guarantee that these magnificent breeds thrive in our homes, we have discussed the necessity of adequate care, including activity requirements, grooming techniques, common health problems, training strategies, and best feeding practices.

It has been a pleasure to share these thoughts and information with you, and I genuinely hope that this book has been both instructive and pleasant for you. My goal was to pique your interest and assist you in finding a breed that speaks to you and your family, ultimately enhancing your lives with the companionship of a poodle mix.

If this book served its goal and provided you with helpful knowledge, I would appreciate it if you could leave a positive review on Amazon.

Your thoughts and support will not only be extremely appreciated but will also help other readers make informed judgments when looking for the appropriate poodle hybrid for their own households.

Thank you for joining me on this fascinating journey into the world of poodle mixes. May your trip be filled with love, laughter, and special moments with your four-legged companions.